Genocide Literature in Middle and Secondary Classrooms

At the heart of this inquiry into the ethical implications of education reform on reading practices in middle and secondary classrooms, the central question is what is lost, hidden, or marginalized in the name of progress? Drawing on her own experiences as an English teacher during the No Child Left Behind era, the author examines school cultures focused on meeting standards and measurable outcomes. She shows how genocide literature illuminates the ethics of reading and helps teachers and students rethink how literature should be taught in this modern, globalized era and the purposes of education more broadly.

Sarah J. Donovan teaches middle school English in a suburb of Chicago, Illinois, USA, and is an adjunct at DePaul University (Social and Cultural Foundations in Education), USA.

Genocide Literature in Middle and Secondary Classrooms

Rhetoric, Witnessing, and Social Action in a Time of Standards and Accountability

Sarah J. Donovan

Routledge
Taylor & Francis Group
LONDON AND NEW YORK

First published 2017 by Routledge

2 Park Square, Milton Park, Abingdon, Oxfordshire OX14 4RN
52 Vanderbilt Avenue, New York, NY 10017

Routledge is an imprint of the Taylor & Francis Group, an informa business

First issued in paperback 2019

Library of Congress Cataloging-in-Publication Data
Names: Donovan, Sarah J., 1973–
Title: Genocide literature in middle and secondary classrooms : rhetoric, witnessing, and social action in a time of standards and accountability / by Sarah J. Donovan.
Description: New York : Routledge, 2017. | Includes bibliographical references and index.
Identifiers: LCCN 2016013404 | ISBN 9781138657236 (hardback) | ISBN 9781315621470 (ebook)
Subjects: LCSH: Genocide—Study and teaching (Middle school)—Illinois. | Genocide in literature. | Educational law and legislation—Illinois. | Education and state—Illinois.
Classification: LCC HV6322.7 .D66 2017 | DDC 364.15/10712773—dc23
LC record available at https://lccn.loc.gov/2016013404

ISBN: 978-1-138-65723-6 (hbk)
ISBN: 978-1-138-31537-2 (pbk)

Typeset in Bembo
by Apex CoVantage, LLC

Contents

Preface

Many English classes in middle and high schools across America read Holocaust literature. However, in the last decade legislative mandates in nearly twenty states now require the study of genocide and its implications. States labeled "local control states," which have local leaders making decisions about curriculum, have also included genocide in their middle and high school standards. This movement to confront genocide began around the same time No Child Left Behind (NCLB) went into effect and the same time I became a middle school English teacher. This book is about my experiences reading genocide literature with students in a time of standards and accountability.

I look into the ethical implications of education mandates on reading instruction and students' reading experiences. I explore how teachers interpret such mandates and what is emphasized and marginalized in an effort to meet requirements. As we begin the era of the Every Student Succeeds Act (ESSA) with new standards and testing, this book offers a conceptual space for English teachers to imagine an era of English education in which our voices advocate for just reading and assessment practices that will nurture in students a capacity to read and make sense of texts beyond tests, beyond the classroom.

My emphasis in this book is on the reading of genocide literature—the experience of reading words that represent unimaginable suffering and resilience alongside teenagers. My words and classroom stories told here will not capture the complexity and beauty of learning that I witnessed. My descriptions of genocide and genocide literature will fail to express the human suffering that is and continues to be genocide. This is not a book that attempts to explain or compare cases of genocide comprehensively because I do not want English teachers to think they have to be historians or genocide scholars to read genocide literature with students. That said, such resources can enhance and complicate literary texts, so I draw upon and reference genocide survivors and scholars throughout this book and encourage teachers and students to consult such experts when questions emerge.

Because the mandate that began this project was a mandate to include "other acts of genocide across the globe" (i.e., "other" than the Holocaust),

I share my classroom experiences reading literature that represents genocide and crimes against humanity in the following cases: Native Peoples of North America, Armenians, Cambodia, Guatemala, Bosnia and Herzegovina, Kosovo, Rwanda, and Sudan. I also include literature suggestions for representations of the Middle Passage, the famine in Ukraine, and the Iraqi Kurds. There are additional genocides that I do not address in this book because of space, the availability of young adult literature on these genocides, and out of ignorance. To scholars of genocide and authors of young adult literature, I hope to learn about your work or inspire you to write about crimes against humanity mentioned here and those I still silence: America's invasion of Mexico, the millions killed in the Philippine-American War, the Congo, Chechnya, Bali, Indonesia, Biafra, East Pakistan, Burundi, East Timor, Paraguay, Bangladesh, Sri Lanka, Bengal, North Korea, Nanking, and the Herrero of Namibia.

I bring to the reader a tremendous diversity of teachable texts. I have spent more than a decade looking for and reading genocide literature; still, I am discovering new, important contributions every year that I add to my classroom library. The books I reference are all books that I have read with my middle school students or colleagues have read with high school students—far more than you can read or teach. Some of these books I consider problematic, but that is not to say that students should not read them. As English teachers, we have a responsibility to teach our students how to read all texts critically, recognizing how the text is working on our hearts and minds including its treatment of human subjects. If you plan to include any of the suggested books in your classroom library, please read them ahead of time so that you can not only make appropriate recommendations but so that you can support your students in their reading experience.

I tell stories from my own classroom in which I have made mistakes and in which I believe I have done some good. I include voices from teachers who have read genocide literature alongside students and from students who allowed me to share their projects, writing, and discussions of genocide literature. While I have sometimes condensed student remarks or corrected grammar, the authenticity of student writing, reactions, perspectives, and developing insights provide direct and valuable evidence of learning processes in the study of genocide literature.

Overview

In Chapter 1, I introduce myself, my classroom, and my school to provide the context for the genesis of this project. Chapter 2 illustrates the ways I saw the state working to standardize and make efficient reading and literature. As part of the institution, I admit that I was complicit in teaching reading and genocide in rather narrow ways. Chapters 3 and 4 explain my research into rhetoric and witnessing and suggest these can be the foundation on which teachers can reconnect with what brought them to teaching

English and shape reading instruction in this new era of reform. Chapter 5 explores the rhetoric and aesthetic of fiction in genocide novels, and the three subsequent chapters—Chapters 6, 7, and 8—demonstrate rhetorical readings of three young adult genocide novels.

In the final section, I share stories from my classroom of how, within a system of standards and accountability, I have tried to shape the use of standards and resist measurement-based structures. Chapter 9 is about writing memoirs as a practice of bearing witness; Chapter 10 focuses on reading a whole-class genocide novel, writing multigenre research papers, and organizing social action; Chapter 11 discusses reading genocide novels independently and in book groups; and Chapter 12 addresses assessing reading without scores or grades. In Chapter 13, I offer some concluding thoughts on reading genocide literature and teaching English in this new era of standards and accountability.

Acknowledgments

First and foremost, thank you to the young people who have read stories alongside me for more than a decade. Your compassion and courage to witness our world is inspiring. I am especially grateful to these students and their families who have trusted me with their writing and allowed me to quote them in this book: Joseph, Gabriela, Mackenzie, Jessica, Rachel, Rebecca, Alejandro, Johnny, Daniel, and David. I hope I have honored your voices.

To my teachers—David Schaafsma, Todd DeStigter, Robert Johnston, and Kate Manski—you have made it possible for me to write this book with your faithful mentoring.

My gratitude goes to the inspiring teachers who have trusted me with their stories, advanced my thinking, and allowed me to quote them in this book. A special thanks to Diane DuBois, my mentor and friend, who witnessed my journey firsthand. Thank you to René Carranza, Jeannette Sander, and Matt Warren for the ultimate gift a principal can give: trust. For your editing skills and encouragement, thank you Jaime Lewandowski, my *hermanita*, and Debbie Gipson.

My sincere appreciation to the scholars who have made contributions to this project with their research and recommendations: Shoshana Felman, Jory Brass, Pat Enciso, Allen Webb, Ralph Cintron, Robert Yagelski, Mark Canuel, Wendy Hesford, Jennifer Berne, Hasan Nuhanović, Mark Barnes, and Debbie Reese; to the outstanding authors of genocide literature, especially Patricia McCormick and Marsha Skrypuch, who have commented on my analyses of their work in addition to illuminating for me their experiences writing and publishing genocide literature; and to the organizations that were instrumental in bringing this book to fruition. Denise Woltering-Vargas of the Stone Center for Latin American Studies helped with my chapter on Guatemala; the Alliance of Universities for Democracy (AUDEM) introduced me to the people of Sarajevo; and the National Council of Teachers of English (NCTE) invited me to share genocide literature with teachers across the country.

Despite nearly a decade of research and writing with all this help, I am sure this book still has shortcomings—those are my fault entirely.

Finally, to my husband, Dan Donovan, thank you for being a witness to my life.

Part I

Mandates

1 The Education of a Teacher

The First Year

I grew up in a middle-class family just outside Chicago, the ninth of eleven children. As a kid, I played with Barbie dolls and tried the sports my older siblings played like soccer and softball, never really finding my niche. In elementary school, I ran for class vice president and later secretary of the student council but never won; I was not popular. I practiced my penmanship diligently so that I could earn the right to use a pen and developed a callous that still reminds me today. In middle school, my father lost his job and never really worked again. While we continued to live in the same neighborhood, we were, in essence, living below the poverty line and surviving on donations from our Catholic church. I spent most nights lying awake watching anywhere from three to five of my ten siblings sleeping in bedrolls on the floor around me. We could not afford beds, nor would the number we needed even fit in the three bedrooms of our small home. When I did sleep, I would often sleepwalk and talk in my dreams, never able to fully rest my mind or body. Despite the size of my family, eight girls and three boys, and even though my father was unemployed for most of my childhood, in many ways, it was typical, white-bread Americana with church on Sundays, park district sports, roller skating through the neighborhood, family dinners, and certainly sibling rivalry (especially over boys).

But there were differences. In a family of eleven, the odds were with us. We learned about teen pregnancy and adoption firsthand. We learned about discrimination on the basis of sexual orientation firsthand. We learned about mental illness firsthand. And we learned about divorce firsthand. I learned all these life lessons as a teenager, so I considered myself somewhat well-informed on social issues and even poverty. While working my way through college, I studied sociology and later worked as a counselor in a jail for a number of years, where I had the privilege of listening to hundreds of life stories—usually through security glass in jail visiting rooms, virtually all of which included tough early-school experiences. I later became a teacher, hoping to teach with and learn from the power of stories, which brought me to Lincoln Junior High School (pseudonym) in 2004 for my first teaching job. I entered the teaching profession in the early years of No Child Left Behind when school districts were scrambling to design systems to close the "achievement gap," the disparity in academic performance between groups of students based on income, race, language, and ability. I could not have anticipated that the stories that helped me make sense of my world and the stories I had hoped to read and write alongside my students would be gradually pushed aside in a march toward higher test scores and that I would be complicit.

Teaching English with NCLB and Data-Driven Instruction

I began teaching middle school English in the fall of 2004 at Lincoln Junior High School. What I found, at least on first impression, was that Lincoln was situated in a middle-class community much like where I grew up. However, there were physical and social signs of change. I was joining Lincoln as an aspect of the district's plan to respond to the school's changing demographics, which was to hire more bilingual staff and ESL-certified teachers and integrate ESL methods in mainstream classrooms.

Lincoln educated the children from the neighborhood, who were mostly white, and children from neighboring elementary schools. The demographics of Lincoln changed so quickly in the early 2000s that the school purchased trailers for the expanding ESL program. Many veteran Lincoln teachers who had taught middle-class European Americans for decades were unfamiliar with strategies to support new Lincoln students' linguistic, cultural, and economic needs. My credentials were quite different from those of the majority of the faculty at the time. I had training in ESL methods, could speak Spanish fairly well, and had a lot of experience working with low-income families in my social work career and graduate assistantship teaching ESL in Chicago's Little Village. Given the demographic shift, I was surprised that the two in-service days preceding the first day of school in 2004 were spent looking at data rather than talking about the linguistic, social, and economic needs of our changing school community.

The first English department meeting of the school year was part of the in-service. We met in room H103, the department chair's classroom. English teachers flipped through class rosters with test scores from the previous school year's state exam, the Illinois Standards Achievement Test (ISAT). As I looked around the room of a dozen or so teachers furiously highlighting away, I quickly grabbed a highlighter, intent to look like I knew what I was doing. I was told to highlight the students who were "on the bubble." Noticing my confusion, Diane, the department head who later became a good friend, explained that a student "on the bubble" meant that the student did not "meet" standards on ISAT but was within a few points of "meeting." In other words, "bubble kids" had the potential to actually pass the ISAT test this year if we "targeted" them. When I asked about all the other students who were below these cutoff scores, she essentially said that they were too far below in reading to bring them up to grade level in one year and that the administration had directed department chairs to concentrate on the "bubble kids." I went to work in silence, remembering advice from my student teaching experience: "Do more listening than speaking." I listened (and highlighted).

What did it mean to "target" a student? I was told that, once identified, "bubble kids" would need extra attention until the March ISAT test in order to raise their ISAT scores, and the "district-approved" curriculum, which would help me target the skills those students needed, was primarily a textbook aligned to the Illinois State Standards. Students below the bubble would benefit, too, but many of those students would also be placed in an additional reading intervention class.

My department chair went on to explain what was at stake. In 2001, No Child Left Behind (NCLB) was signed into law. School districts were scrambling to meet the requirements of NCLB, specifically the requirement that 100 percent of students must "meet" on their state reading and math tests by the year 2013–2014. Essentially, NCLB redefined the federal role in K–12 education to close the achievement gap between students at the lower end of the performance scale (referring to minority, low-income students) and those performing better (typically middle-class white students). Federal funding for schools was soon based on student achievement. If any achievement gaps were identified through the testing process, the school district had to address those issues with a plan for improvement. If schools did not perform and close the achievement gap identified by their state assessment, they risked losing federal funding and being "taken over" or "turned around" by the government. Due to Lincoln's changing demographics, the district had a lot at stake in the early years of NCLB. Using the ISAT data to drive instruction and target achievement gaps so that we did not leave children behind sounded pretty good to me at the time.

I did not know the first thing about teaching English from data, using research-based lesson plans, or following a textbook's scope and sequence. Thinking back to my own learning experiences with high-stakes tests, I couldn't recall a single time that teachers asked me to look at my scores and set a goal for improving my reading or math scores. Maybe I was "targeted" and did not know it. Still, I do not remember test prep lessons for what was the Iowa Basic Skills in my schooling, but I do remember test anxiety and comparing test results with my siblings (and feeling quite inadequate). And my teacher education courses did not prepare me for the data collection or goal-setting lessons I would have to create with my students, nor did it prepare me for displaying data charts on my bulletin boards as a transparent accountability measure. What I was prepared to do was to develop conceptual units of study with primary sources and authentic writing experiences. I was prepared to provide narrative feedback and assess with portfolios. I had learned that the classroom walls should be covered with student writing and inspiration. The "good news" was that I did not have to spend my nights and weekends developing such units; the school district had purchased everything I needed, and all this was waiting for me in my classroom: G109. I just had to follow the teacher's guide.

I was presented a district-approved textbook written by Who Knows and published by Prentice Hall, a Pearson Education company that offered "research-based" textbooks. I was given the silver level for my "regular classes" (students at or below grade level in reading) and the gold level for my "gifted" class (students reading above grade level). The Pearson textbook package included CDs with recordings of every text (mostly excerpts from primary sources such as Maya Angelou's *I Know Why the Caged Bird Sings* or Daniel Keyes's *Flowers for Algernon*), VHS tapes for "anticipatory activities," a database for test questions, three levels of consumables (e.g., workbooks for on-level readers, adapted versions for those below level, and even an ESL version), and skills worksheets with every graphic organizer imaginable. Clearly, the district had invested significantly in not leaving any child behind. I did not know where to begin, so I took everything home and began making sense of it all—two days.

That year, and for a few years more, the classrooms and hallways were covered with data charts and mission statements to raise reading and math scores. I had students charting their reading scores and setting improvement goals. I posted lists grouping students by skill deficits: word analysis, literary works, literary devices, and comprehension. As a department, we "targeted" students by identifying a deficit, teaching to the deficit, and then assessing for growth. At one point in my first year, Lincoln even had visitors from other schools and districts to see how we were using data to drive instruction. (The year prior, our district won a prestigious quality award for corporate and social responsibility.) The visitors were mesmerized by my charts: weekly word analysis charts, comprehension competitions, and reading scores from quarter to quarter. These graphics were what our school called "quality tools" designed to troubleshoot quality-related issues: fishbones, check sheets, Pareto charts, scatter diagrams, and histograms. All teachers were encouraged to use these tools. I certainly did, and I was proud of it.

As a novice teacher, I did not understand why teachers complained about being underappreciated. The district office was visiting classrooms and celebrating teachers for their efforts. It seemed like teachers were literally shining a light on the students who had been or would be "left behind" had we not looked at the data. It seemed like we were targeting their needs and filling them. There were, however, always students below the "bubble." And when those charts were posted for the school (and visitors) to see, a student knew which dot scattered in this or that quadrant represented her.

Year after year, students who did not "meet standards" on the state test received more interventions, an additive approach to improvement. When goal setting did not work, students were placed in an intervention class and tested more frequently. The intervention classes were often expensive scripted programs stating what to teach, when to teach it, and how to teach it. Such curriculum has been dubbed "teacher-proof" curriculum. After all, when a child is in a school for a number of years and does not pass the test, the school must makes changes where it can: the curriculum and the teacher. I think that by hiring me, Lincoln was showing cultural and linguistic progress, and I think that by buying the Prentice Hall curriculum, Lincoln was showing progress with research-based materials, and, certainly, the "quality tools" represented the image of a cutting-edge education. However, in the name of progress, a typical junior high student below the bubble did not have room in her schedule for music, art, language, or technology classes. She spent her day in two math classes, three language arts classes, one science class, one history class, and one resource class (i.e., homework and linguistic support). In the name of progress, the potential of instruction to be guided by teachers, students' stories, and discovery was neutralized by the specter of the test and fear of failing to meet.

Even though I did not have to develop my own curriculum and had access to many "quality tools," that first year of teaching was not easy. When I wasn't looking at charts, I was trying to figure out the district-approved curriculum; I was overwhelmed by the graphic organizers, worksheets, and step-by-step teacher guides. Six eighth-grade groups of students came to me each day for forty-one minutes of reading or writing. We worked on labeling Freytag's plot triangle and identifying the main idea, author's purpose, and literary devices in texts—skills most students had been learning since third grade. While we did read short stories, poems, plays, and essays, we read them out of a five-pound textbook. And while we did discuss some works by Edgar Allan Poe, Sir Arthur Conan Doyle, Naomi Shihab Nye, Langston Hughes, and Walter Dean Myers, such discussions were guided by the manual and prompted by questions at the end of the text. We did not curl up with a good book on a papasan chair or beanbag like I imagined when I was in my teacher education classes. Such a luxury would have interrupted our "progress."

Even though most of these kids had been in our district for their entire education, being carefully monitored in the data, by the time they reached junior high, students' reading levels ranged from second grade to high school. The systems of progress were failing many students, and it seemed quite apparent that the categories of students failing were in two of NCLB's subgroups: low income and English language learners. NCLB required that 100 percent of students meet its Academic Yearly Progress goals, and that includes 100 percent of the subgroups. Subgroups are defined by race, socioeconomic status (i.e., students who receive free or reduced-priced meals), special education, and English learners. Increasingly more of Lincoln's students were represented in the low-income and English learners subgroups.

Two Mandates Intersect: NCLB and Genocide Education

The fall of 2005 was the start of my second year of teaching and, once again, I sat in H103 with the English department doing data analysis. I was quiet and learned to stay quiet after finding, or being assigned, my place in the faculty hierarchy. Diane passed around some welcome-back brownies and said that we needed ideas on two topics. According to the 2004 ISAT data, our students scored lowest on inferencing questions, so we would have to develop a system for targeting inferencing. Apparently, inferencing was the English teacher's nemesis. How does one teach inferencing well?

> "Maybe we could develop a PowerPoint on inferencing," one teacher suggested.
>
> "Maybe we should test this skill weekly and assess the data," suggested another.

We were fairly certain there was some worksheet on inferencing in the Prentice Hall materials. Most of us agreed, however, that inferencing is not easily measured by multiple-choice questions, and the ISAT is a multiple-choice test. Then Diane continued with the second item on our agenda: We also had to do some curriculum planning for a new mandate. Our curriculum was essentially Prentice Hall, so we were puzzled, but then Diane explained that the curriculum we would be planning was for a new unit on genocide. Groans came from every direction in H103.

Diane explained that in June Illinois became the first state in the nation to end state investment (to divest) in Sudan because Colin Powell declared the atrocities in Darfur "genocide." At that time, I could not have pointed to Sudan on a map, and I could not have defined genocide. Based on the facial expressions of the other teachers, they couldn't either. She went on to explain that in August, just weeks before school started, Illinois's House and Senate enacted Public Act 094-0478, the Illinois Genocide Curriculum Mandate, requiring all Illinois public schools to include "an additional unit of instruction studying other acts of genocide across the globe." This mandate was an amendment to Illinois's Holocaust Education Mandate enacted in 1990. In addition to learning about the genocide in Sudan, Diane explained, students would learn about the Armenian Genocide, the forced famine in Ukraine, and other more recent atrocities in Cambodia, Bosnia, and Rwanda. Here is an excerpt from the press release written by Illinois's then governor, Rod Blagojevich:

> As we teach our kids the important lessons of history, we have to be sure that they understand that racial, national, ethnic and religious hatred can lead to horrible tragedies. Sadly, these are not just the problems of our parents' or grandparents' generations. We have to make sure our schools teach the importance of embracing differences among people and encourage students to fight intolerance and hatred wherever they see it. ("Gov. Blagojevich Signs Law")

On my desk were printouts of data, numbers that indicated students' lack of inferencing skills, and alongside this was an announcement, a mandate, that schools will teach "the importance of embracing differences" and encourage "students to fight intolerance and hatred." At the time, I was wondering about how I could teach inferencing in the genocide unit. Indeed, inferencing is quite important when it comes to deciphering genocide intent: In the absence of direct evidence, genocide intent can be inferred from circumstantial evidence. I was not, however, thinking of this. I was thinking about how to improve test scores. The irony of teaching genocide with data-driven instruction or attempting to quantify some understanding of genocide had *not*, at the time, occurred to me. The state was putting students into groups by their race, culture, class, language, and ability. Teachers were asked to target those students so that they could perform better on a state test. And now, the state was mandating that we teach about genocide, the intent to systematically eliminate racial, ethnic, religious, linguistic, and cultural groups of human beings. How did one measure the ability to embrace differences and fight intolerance? What would that test look like? How would I "target" a low score on intolerance?

The mandate emerged out of a well-intended sense of moral outrage at the crimes against humanity in Sudan, but like most mandates, it felt like more work for teachers. No content or standard was going to be removed to make space for something new, which meant we would have to cut out or rush through other units; we would have to find the materials and create the lesson plans. Because it was an unfunded mandate, we would have to use our department funds to buy genocide literature, which meant we would need to read literature about genocides and decide, together, what was appropriate for our students and what was worth buying with our precious department money. The greatest concern, however, was that this new mandate came at a time when testing was replacing teaching time, and test scores were used to evaluate teachers, track subgroups, and rate schools.

The junior high English teachers at Lincoln responded to this mandate in a variety of ways: a sigh, a rolling of the eyes, a "what is genocide" whisper, and a "yes, important" comment. As a group, however, we questioned why we, the English department, were discussing it and not the history department, to which Diane responded that our curriculum had more space for this added unit. It seemed to her that since we were able to find some great literature to teach the Holocaust in our English classes, we would be able to find some great literature about these genocides, which sounded logical. Indeed, I had taught a unit on the Holocaust the previous year with help from the department and the textbook. The Holocaust unit was in April after ISATs. I was woefully unprepared to discuss unimaginable atrocities with eighth graders after having spent the first half of the year thinking about data. The Prentice Hall literature textbook included Goodrich and Hackett's dramatic adaptation of *The Diary of Anne Frank* complete with lesson plans, which was a big help, but the publishers clearly had not anticipated this additional genocide unit in their standards-aligned, research-based textbook.

Conclusion

Any veteran teacher will tell you that education initiatives come and go. Some resonate with teachers more than others, and some have more staying power. Teachers have learned to go with such initiatives (or appear to anyway). This mandate resonated with me, stirred something in me. I was hearing an opportunity to think about how the world, our world, was changing. Clearly, Lincoln was changing. I was part of that change, but this 2005 mandate reiterated the need for a cultural, political, and even moral education that I was not so sure we were ready for. Instead of skill acquisition as a way of participating in this world, the mandate asked us to teach a way of being, participating, and shaping the world. There was no textbook for that. No research-based curriculum. No test. It was up to us to do the inquiry into the topic and figure out a way to make it accessible to junior high students. The genocide mandate offered an opportunity to think about and talk about something other than goal setting, testing, and data analysis or rather to talk about such measurement practices and how they are, in fact, leaving kids behind.

Works Cited

"Gov. Blagojevich Signs Law Expanding Genocide Education in Illinois: Studies Will Now Include Recent Atrocities in Armenia, Ukraine, Cambodia, Bosnia, Rwanda and Sudan." News. Springfield: Office of the Governor, 2005. Web.

"Illinois General Assembly—Full Text of Public Act 094-0478." *Illinois General Assembly Home Page*. 24 Apr. 2011. Web.

"Illinois Genocide Curriculum Mandate." http://www.genocideeducationnetwork.org/. Web.

Prentice Hall: Timeless Voices, Timeless Themes, Silver Level. Upper Saddle River, NJ: Prentice Hall, 2002. Print.

2 Reading and Meeting a Mandate to Study Genocide

To teach about genocide means to call attention to the question of how much power a state should have (e.g., state sovereignty), the responsibility of a community to put humanity over political and economic issues, and the ethics of every institution that contributes to the development of a nation that recognizes only certain groups of people. To learn about genocide means teachers and students need to read stories from beyond the pages of our content anthologies and learn to listen to voices that will trouble what it means to demonstrate growth and account for progress. To teach genocide means to think about the social forces that create the need for initiatives like NCLB and genocide education acts. I was not ready to do that in my second year of teaching. I did not know how to even begin.

In 2005, when Illinois mandated a unit of instruction on genocide in all public schools, it fell to the English teachers at Lincoln to develop the curriculum to meet this mandate with no training or financial support. What follows is a description of how this new curriculum policy was implemented at Lincoln from my point of view. It is not a comprehensive study but rather my account of how I and the teachers who agreed to share their stories with me taught about genocide at a time when we felt increasing pressure to help our school make Adequate Yearly Progress (AYP), the measure by which schools were held accountable for student performance. This first year of the Illinois Genocide Education Mandate at Lincoln is the basis on which the rest of this book builds because it was only in considering how I taught about genocide then that I began to understand the potential and imperative of the English classroom now as the Every Student Succeeds Act (ESSA) replaces NCLB.

The account that follows demonstrates how the state's vision of education has muddled the potential of English to nurture in students a capacity for understanding our diverse world and their place in it. In other words, the obsession with data and testing represented one kind of vision of progress—a vision of data, measurement, and achievement—while the genocide mandate represented the opportunity to pursue a different kind of vision—recognition of how progress represents and perpetuates discrimination and violence.

First, we'll take a look at how the genocide mandate came about. I think it is important to step outside the classroom to understand how the genocide education mandate came to pass. I will take a close look at the language of the 2005 mandate and consider how the language speaks to the intention of Illinois legislators considering political, economic, and educational dimensions. Then I will describe Lincoln's genocide curriculum development and implementation.

Inside the Legislative Process

Originally filed January 19, 2005, House Bill 312 was enacted just seven months later on August 5, 2005. The Illinois School Code was thus amended to read that every public and elementary school shall include a "unit of instruction" studying the events of the Holocaust and "an additional unit of instruction studying other acts of genocide" ("Illinois Genocide Curriculum Mandate").

If we turn to the text of the mandate to teach a unit of instruction on genocide, we see it begins with the original wording from the 1990 mandate to teach a unit of instruction on the Holocaust: "One of the lessons of the Holocaust is that national, ethnic, racial or religious hatred can overtake any nation or society, leading to calamitous consequences." The text indicates that the reason to make teaching about the Holocaust a mandate, to amend the school code as such, is to serve as a "reaffirmation of the commitment of free peoples from all nations to never again permit the occurrence of another Holocaust" ("Illinois Genocide Curriculum Mandate"). This is a public declaration by Illinois legislators to Illinois schools (who read the school code) that the Illinois Congress is taking a position and, hence, Illinois public schools shall, too. But a mandate to teach about the Holocaust has existed since 1990. For fifteen years leading up to this 2005 amendment, schools were, presumably, reaffirming the commitment to "never again" allow another Holocaust. And yet here we have the need for another public declaration.

We will see how this bit of legislation rhetorically works to condemn the authoritarian state of Sudan and intervene in state violence that threatens individual freedom, inciting economic and humanitarian action (e.g., divesting in Sudan and teaching about genocide in schools) rather than military action. To be clear, I am asserting that a school code amendment functions rhetorically; words are trying to act upon schools, teachers, and students, to write upon them a way of knowing about the world. What readers fail to notice when responding to such a text is the problem the new policy is attempting to redress. What is in the gap between the first amendment to the school code and the second: the Holocaust mandate and genocide mandate, NCLB and ESSA? Why make the amendment now? How will words change the state of things?

It is important to reiterate what I noted earlier, that prior to the debate about House Bill 312, there was a debate on the Illinois Senate floor about divestment from Sudan on May 17, 2005. Senate Bill 23 was an Act to End Atrocities and Terrorism in Sudan. This bill aimed to "prohibit any state monies from being invested in any entity associated with the Republic of Sudan" (6). It was in this meeting that Rep. Jack Franks reported details on the genocide in Sudan to the House referencing Ruth Messinger's article "Hotel Darfur." In this title, Messinger alludes to the film *Hotel Rwanda* to make a comparison between the Rwandan Genocide, in which 800,000 people of the Tutsi minority were massacred, and the escalating crisis in Darfur: "World leaders knew; our government knew, and did nothing" (Messinger 1). Rep. Franks knew, too, and he took the House floor to take a stand on the record. The transcript from the 94th General Assembly provides a sociopolitical context for House Bill 312 and content for the mandated "unit of instruction" about genocide. Franks states:

> 2,000,000 African tribal farmers have been violently driven from their homes by the government of Sudan and the militias they named . . . called Janjaweed. Despite repeated calls . . . from humanitarian organizations and United States agencies warning of the worst humanitarian crises in the world today, there continues to be a systematic program of expulsion, rape and murderous violence that has taken at least 300,000 lives since the crisis began in February 2003 . . . Recently, Jews all over the world remembered the consequences of inaction by the international community in the face of genocide. We remember and we still cannot, nor will we ever, comprehend how the world looked on as 6,000,000 Jews were gassed, tortured, displaced, starved and worked to death. And we vowed never again! So we must all be the guardians of this call for action, highly sensitive and responsive to all attempts by any people to annihilate another people. The world stood by idly 60 years ago, and again as massacres unfolded in Cambodia, Rwanda, and now Sudan.
>
> ("State of Illinois 94th General Assembly House of Representatives Transcription Debate 51st Legislative Day")

This sentiment of "never again" was reinforced in the genocide education mandate. In addition to pointing out the lessons available in this curriculum and the "reaffirmation," this bill also sought to recognize that "crimes of genocide continue to be perpetrated across the globe as they have been in the past" and "to deter indifference to crimes against humanity and human suffering wherever they may occur" ("Illinois Genocide Curriculum Mandate"). Rep. Franks referenced the United States' response when he said, "And we vowed never again!" The vow is in President Truman's signature on the Convention on the Prevention and Punishment of the Crime of Genocide of 1948, an international treaty that was not ratified by the U.S. Senate until 1986. The list of genocides suggested in Public Act 094-0478 includes the Armenian Genocide, the famine-genocide in Ukraine, and more recent atrocities in Cambodia, Bosnia, Rwanda, and Sudan. By naming specific occurrences of genocide, the lawmakers privilege the knowledge of certain genocides, crimes against humanity, and human rights violations while continuing to silence others: Native Peoples of North Americas, slavery, the invasion of Mexico, the Philippines-American War, the Congo, refusing to admit Jewish refugees, Guatemala, El Salvador, Argentina, East Timor, Iraqi Kurds, and still others that I again silence here. The United States was complicit in many of these situations, which is, perhaps, why these genocides were not named in the mandate and why the U.S. delayed ratifying the international treaty against genocide.

The Convention committed the United States to prevent and punish acts of genocide. A "contracting party" in this convention agrees that "genocide, conspiracy to commit genocide, direct and public incitement to commit genocide, attempt to commit genocide and complicity in genocide is punishable" ("Convention on the Prevention"). A "contracting party" also agrees to prevent genocide. Still, the U.S. did not intervene in the 1994 genocide in Rwanda or the 1995 Srebrenica massacre. Promises, mandates, and signatures alone do not bring about change. Where is the social action?

Illinois is not the only state with a mandate to teach genocide. Many states have a legislative mandate requiring schools to teach a unit on the Holocaust and "other acts of genocide," while some without a mandate require Holocaust and genocide education in the state learning standards. Still, there are some states that leave curriculum decisions to local school districts to decide how best to meet the standards, which invites opportunities to explore genocide and its implications.

At a time when the national education movement was indeed globally aware in the democratic sense of development, progress, and competition with other nations, the rhetoric of the genocide mandate, and I mean the actual text of this mandate, was highlighting a consequence of such development. While indeed mandating a topic of instruction, which was a part of the official discourse teachers had come to expect, the language of the mandate deviated from language of competition, skills, and achievement by asking for an awareness of global atrocities and doing so without stipulating how to teach it or measure it. The genocide mandate complicates the public discourse of education because it does not ask for progress in the quantitative sense; it asks for teachers to raise awareness of unimaginable human suffering caused by the actions and inaction of human beings and their institutions. The Illinois legislators were not telling teachers to teach about mass murder but rather "genocide," a systematic, complex process that is planned, coordinated, and rationalized according to state and national ideologies.

Still, the teachers sitting in H103 that August morning in 2005, including me, were not terribly interested in the legislative process of the mandate nor open to making connections between genocide and education reform. They were thinking: How long does the unit have to be? What do we have to teach? And when will we fit this in?

Meeting the Mandate: Developing the Curriculum

Knowing that it was up to teachers to develop the curriculum to meet the genocide mandate, I joined the Genocide Curriculum Committee for our district, which consisted of a group of interested elementary teachers, two junior high English teachers, and one junior high history teacher. Over a few summer days, we developed curriculum for grades five through eight, which included lists of important vocabulary, key concepts, and collections of articles, stories, and films. We then collected all the materials in a binder to be distributed at the beginning of the school year.

Starting in fifth grade, teachers would explore concepts such as tolerance, responsibility, and empathy. Students might read picture books about the Holocaust and/or select longer works such as *Daniel's Story*, *Touch Wood: A Girlhood in Occupied France*, *Lisa's War*, *Friedrich*, and *Number the Stars*. Sixth grade would consider world leaders and leadership styles according to historical periods they studied and continue reading from the elementary Holocaust book list. An extension might include the concept of "agents of change" and stories about children in war-torn countries. For the most part, the committee recommended materials to supplement or extend units already in place in elementary classrooms.

For junior high, the committee considered the list of suggested genocides provided in the mandate, for we knew of no others: the Armenian Genocide, the famine-genocide in Ukraine, Cambodia, Bosnia, Rwanda, and Sudan. We divided the listed genocides by grade level using the history textbook as a guide. Because eighth-grade history taught about World Wars I and II and the Vietnam War and because eighth-grade English teachers had taught about the Holocaust since 1990, we assigned Turkey's genocide of Armenians and the Cambodian genocide to eighth grade. We researched literature, read reviews, and ordered class sets of *The Forgotten Fire* by Adam Bagdasarian, a novel about the Armenian Genocide, and *First They Killed My Father* by Loung Ung, a memoir about the Cambodian genocide (see Chapter 9). We had not, however, read either. There were few options, but the reviews for these two were good; the Lexiles were appropriate for junior high; and they offered genre diversity. In doing research for young-adult novels for junior high after the committee adjourned, I discovered other genocide novels, but one I purchased with my own money for students at Lincoln: *Tree Girl* by Ben Mikaelsen. It is about the genocide in Guatemala in the early 1980s, which was not mentioned in the Illinois mandate, I suspect, because of the U.S. involvement (see Chapter 10).

Seventh grade, which already had a unit on current events, was assigned Rwanda. We were limited to what was available at the time, and not many young-adult novels had been written about Rwanda in 2005, so we bought the film *Hotel Rwanda*. More current than Rwanda was Sudan, so that was assigned to the seventh-grade English teachers. We bought the 2004 documentary *The Lost Boys of Sudan* directed by Megan Mylan to help teachers and students explore the conflict in Sudan. Because Bosnia was within the decade and still rather current, Lincoln bought a class set of *Zlata's Diary* for seventh-grade English teachers to explore the Siege of Sarajevo (1992–1996), but they would have to teach about Srebrenica (1995) using other materials. (I have still not found a young-adult novel that tells the story of Srebrenica.) While we had some difficulty locating memoirs or even historical fiction about the Ukraine famine (1932), we were able to find some resources so that seventh-grade teachers could consider social engineering and antecedents to Stalin's manmade famine. Thinking about this now, the forced famine seems to fit better in the eighth-grade curriculum leading up to the Holocaust given Hitler's relationship with Stalin, but I did not know about it at the time, and no one else suggested it.

Essentially, the curriculum committee used chronology to divide up the responsibility of meeting the mandate and developed a sequence of instruction in each grade level and subject. Our district gave us time to work on this and offered some funding for materials and a conference. They trusted their teachers. We relied on our experience and summer research to develop the curriculum at the time, not having read or viewed all the materials we were considering nor having taught any of it ourselves. The committee worked as an extension of the state, assigning content, materials, and accountability to meet the mandate. It would be up to teachers to use their discipline training to make use of the materials the committee gathered.

Implementing the Genocide Curriculum in Stages

In 2006, the first year of implementing the plan the curriculum committee developed for the "additional unit on genocide," the seventh-grade teams—all the English teachers including math, history, science, special education, and ELL teachers—created an interdisciplinary unit I which they (teachers and students) watched *Hotel Rwanda*, learned about the stages of genocide from Gregory Stanton, and developed posters or PowerPoints in small groups with factual information and images.

Students and teachers were organized by what they called "learning stations." One teacher took a station and facilitated a project based on that station's genocide. This was organized during the final two weeks of school, a time strategically selected because this was after ISATs and the final MAP tests (a computerized reading and math tests administered by our school district three times a year).

The first year this unit was implemented in the eighth grade, there was no team-wide effort. The history department "covered" genocide chronologically as it fit with their textbook, and then the English teachers approached the unit as an extension of the Holocaust unit. Some teachers chose not to teach an additional unit on genocide the first year, having not had time to read through the new curriculum that the genocide committee developed, but all taught the Holocaust, which they had been teaching for quite a few years by now. For the teachers willing to try teaching about genocide, the most common modification made to the Holocaust unit was the inclusion of Gregory Stanton's eight stages of genocide: classification, symbolization, dehumanization, organization, polarization, preparation, extermination, and denial. After applying the eight stages to the Holocaust as a model, students were then assigned a genocide from the list and applied the stages. For example, symbolization in the Holocaust included naming people "Jews" or "Gypsies" or distinguishing them by colors or dress such as the yellow star for Jews under Nazi rule. Similarly, the people from the Eastern Zone in Khmer Rouge, Cambodia, were forced to wear a blue scarf. The rationale behind the stages, according to Stanton, is this:

> Genocide is a process that develops in eight stages that are predictable but not inexorable. At each stage, preventive measures can stop it. The process is not linear. Logically, later stages must be preceded by earlier stages. But all stages continue to operate throughout the process.
>
> (Stanton)

In the classroom, the stage approach to genocide education included students' filling out a graphic organizer for their assigned genocide to indicate stages from classification through denial based on the texts they read or movies they watched. My students identified these stages for Guatemala using Mikaelsen's *Tree Girl*, for the Armenian Genocide using Bagdasarian's *Forgotten Fire*, and for Cambodia using Ung's *First They Killed My Father.* If a visitor stopped by Lincoln's classrooms post–ISATs, she might see posters about the eight stages of genocide, vocabulary cubes, or even newsletters that discussed the stages of genocide.

The frame of Gregory Stanton's "Eight Stages of Genocide" appealed to me and other teachers because stage identification is a neat mechanism for making genocide accessible to students (and teachers). Each stage shows how genocide is preventable and prompts discussion about what the international community did or could have done to intervene. However, the stages misled students into thinking genocide can be so easily understood. Used as the only mechanism for understanding genocide, the stages conflate the complexity of genocide and minimize the multitude of stories that help us understand the institutions and ideologies that make genocide possible.

The genocide curriculum we created and implemented was not perfect. Placed at the end of the school year, it just felt ancillary and insufficient. Still, without much training or funding, we were raising awareness of genocide and attempting to deter indifference to human suffering. Genocide education is not something that can be covered or met, and learning about genocide is not something that can be quantified or easily measured.

The Darker Side of Meeting Mandates

In 2012, after nearly six years of teaching English in the NCLB era, I sat down to talk to a few of Lincoln's English teachers about their experiences teaching about genocide. In these excerpts, teachers share memorable experiences:

DIANE: Well, I remember when we first read *Tree Girl*, how that sucked the air out of the room. And the kids just locked into this idea. It was a big "Aha!" moment for them of what it's like to be someone their age living in this situation. And then, I think the thing that got me the most . . . I don't know why I am crying . . . But after we had done all of this discussion I showed them *Paperclips*. And again, you could just hear a pin drop because they got it. This just gets me.

ELAINE: I had a student actually that her mother was Bosnian. And so, when we were doing the Bosnian genocide, that student brought some of that to life in talking about her mom's family.

DOMINGO: One of my memorable moments was I had a kid write to Senator Obama about the genocide. . . . We got a letter from Senator Barack Obama from Illinois, thanking us for writing about the genocide in Darfur, Sudan. . . . [Students] sort of felt that at some point in life, there might be a change that might be made.

KATIE: [Genocide] gives them a connection that they can relate to like this is the little microcosm in my school of people not treating other people the right way, of people ignoring things and pretending it's not happening when it is, or avoiding situations like that. And then seeing that in a world context where they can kind of relate to that idea that one person or one group breaking down another person or another group while a whole lot of other people kind of stand aside is part of what keeps genocide going . . . because they've all been either the bully, the victim, or a bystander—probably all three a lot of them at some point in time.

Diane speaks of students "getting it"; Elaine uses the phrase "came to life"; Mingo says "there might be a change"; and Katie speaks about "connection" and "world context." The language in these excerpts is the kind of language I'd like to see in school reform. Instead of talk of standards and scores, why aren't we talking about "life" and "change" and "connection" and "world context"? Unfortunately, these conversations happen at the end of the school year, after testing.

Between that first year of implementing genocide education (2006) and the year I interviewed teachers about the mandate (2012), NCLB pressures mounted, and our school failed to meet AYP on the state test several times. Enthusiasm for meeting the genocide mandate waned. Enthusiasm for teaching English waned as well. My passion for teaching English waned so much that in 2010 I took a leave of absence. The time away helped me recognize how NCLB had impacted my teaching, so during my interviews with teachers about the genocide curriculum, I asked teachers about how NCLB has impacted the way they teach English:

DIANE: Probably in the last four years I've done more test prep . . . I think that the time we may have taken to meander off onto things that might have come up as a side conversation, "Oh, let's learn about that"—that is gone . . . I suspect that has to do with wanting to measure up . . . because you know the administration is looking.

ELAINE: For me, I think I just ended up going more the direct teaching, and I think part of it is that I need to cover this, this, and this for ISATs, for MAP testing, and I feel the pressure that I have to cover all of these things; whereas before it was, "Let's talk about the books more, let's talk about the stories more."

KATIE: So, I always feel pressure because I feel like I'm part of a team here at this school. So, as part of that team we have to make sure our school's successful every year. And the title "failing school" is frustrating because I don't want to ever be a failing school. But then I feel like we have to make our kids better test takers. . . . The reading just for the enjoyment of reading kind of gets pushed to the side.

DOMINGO: Personally, I don't feel that the state is on my back to do what I'm expected to do according to the Illinois State Standards. I do adhere to the standards . . . I do implement them in my way in the classroom, so I don't feel restricted . . . looking at the ISAT data, MAP data . . . I feel and I think that data sort of justifies how I'm doing within the classroom.

Some teachers talked about the need to "measure up" and be "part of a team" as they "cover" topics using more "direct teaching" and "test prep." They did not use this language when talking about genocide education. What I heard from some teachers and what I felt myself is that standards and accountability changed the way we saw our role in the English classroom and the school. Now in 2016 with ESSA, schools and teachers are focused on how to best implement the new standards and prepare for the new tests, but I don't want another decade of restrictive practices in which conversations about humanity are pushed to the margins. I want to be a part of shaping how this new era manifests in the English classroom.

Conclusion

In teaching about genocide and talking about genocide education with teachers, I discovered how important ideas and experiences are pushed to the margins of education in the name of progress. The dominant discourse of education, measurement, is deeply invested in a value system that no longer aligns with the sort of education that society needs if education is to respond to the economic, social, technological, political, and environmental changes happening around the world.

The reforms are all about the standardization of learning and efficiency—marks of measurement. Progress, even if it is toward some sort of rationality (which we might see as a just cause like NCLB and not leaving any child behind), ultimately excludes the very ideas that have potential to bring about change. The implications of such accountability measures have led to isolating students from certain learning experiences such as art, language, and music so that students can receive more reading or math instruction. Teachers have felt pressure to cover skills that will be tested, pushing aside reading time and literary discussions in favor of test prep. A mandate like genocide education is seen as something to meet rather than a movement to promote acceptance and social action in schools. Some teachers may see reform as something done *to* them or *to* the students. We may hear teachers complain of the hours spent testing; however, teachers have to recognize that we are part of the institution of education—not separate from it. We do have the power to shape the structures within the institution with our action or inaction. The study of genocide reveals the most severe cases of inaction when time and again the international community, including the United States, did not intervene when confronted with evidence of genocide. So what will be our role in this new era of reform?

We have to change our systems from within. The darker side of reform is its order-making efforts: the procedural rationality, the division of tasks, and the categorization of peoples. All these play a role in education, but they also played a role in the Holocaust and genocide. I am suggesting that in an increasingly globalized world, we cannot afford narrow ways of knowing or narrow ways of teaching. To begin, English teachers have to resist inclinations to order or constrain reading experiences. Our practice must be more inclusive and complex so as to engage students with their world in and beyond the classroom. Reading to recognize the systems that have been deciding for us what is worth knowing and experiencing means reading the way words work on our habits of mind and actions. This book is my journey to reimagine the English classroom with the lessons I learned from my study of genocide.

Works Cited

"Convention on the Prevention and Punishment of the Crime of Genocide." *Prevent Genocide International.* 22 Apr. 2011. Web.

"Illinois General Assembly—Full Text of Public Act 094-0478." *Illinois General Assembly Home Page.* 24 Apr. 2011. Web.

"Illinois Genocide Curriculum Mandate." *Genocide Education Network of Illinois.org.* 24 Apr. 2011. Web.

Messinger, Ruth. "Hotel Darfur." *American Jewish World Service.* May. 2005. Web.

Stanton, Gregory. "The Eight Stages of Genocide." *Genocide Watch.org.* 1998. Web.

"State of Illinois 94th General Assembly House of Representatives Transcription Debate 51st Legislative Day." *Illinois General Assembly.* 17 May 2005. 24 Apr. 2011. Web.

Part II

Rhetoric, Witnessing, and the Witness

3 The Rhetoric of the Word

A Case Study of Bosnia and Herzegovina

> Once we add the context of race and ethnicity into the various definitions of murder, the door to more dramatic definitions opens. Merriam-Webster defines genocide as the killing of people that are part of a political, cultural, or racial group. This seems to be the most open and straightforward definition of genocide. Encyclopedia Britannica's definition requires the murders to be systematic to be labeled genocide. A pogrom requires organized killing of helpless people, usually because of race or religion. And "ethnic cleansing" doesn't necessarily require murder (it can be "removal") but for those displaced it is likely tantamount to both.
>
> —Mallory Moss, "The Language of Genocide"

While language names the beauty and horror in the world, language also constrains, limits, and excludes in the process of naming. As Moss describes, naming an event "murder," "genocide," "pogrom," or "ethnic cleansing" may seem like progress to those doing the naming (or "straightforward"), but for the "helpless people" and "those displaced," there is nothing straightforward about "the language of genocide." As teachers of English, we recognize the power of words to move our hearts and minds, but as I've been arguing in this book, teachers have a responsibility to teach students how to read what words are doing to shape our understanding of the world.

Genocide is not an event that has a beginning and an end. It is an enduring darkness that shades our existence before, during, and long after mass murder. Our nation's attempt to assimilate Native Peoples in early America continues to impact Native communities. The legacy of slavery lives in racially segregated communities, high numbers of African Americans in our prisons, and extrajudicial killings of African Americans by police. Despite Turkey's refusal to name the 1915 massacre of 1.5 million Armenians under the Ottoman Empire a genocide, Armenians are still in U.S. and Turkish courts seeking restitution of assets and property rights. The word names what happened and what is happening but cannot capture all its implications. The word names a condition of humanity.

What I've learned about teaching reading by teaching about genocide is that reading resists measurement and defies time. English teachers first and foremost recognize that texts have a purpose and that their authors are using language to move readers to think, believe, feel, and act. Words attempt to construct a reader's understanding of an idea, an event, a person, and a time in the service of the writer's cause or purpose. Words can purport certain ideas, achieve certain outcomes, and push agendas—sometimes ethical, sometimes not. And English teachers know that words linger beyond the reading event and, thus, have implications.

In this chapter, I explore how people use the past, at times, for their own purposes, manipulating and even creating memories as the means for setting a national agenda. It is here that I make clear that English teachers, teachers of what words can do, are not merely preparing students to earn a good grade or pass a high-stakes test but are preparing students to be members of society who understand how words can serve opposing causes and implicate readers in sometimes unethical agendas. English teachers already work with rhetoric, and the new standards encourage a study of rhetoric, but I suggest teachers move away from identifying rhetorical moves and toward noticing texts as enacting a condition of the human experience. To understand how rhetoric works to impact humanity, English teachers must help students think about reading as something beyond skills or standards toward an inquiry into how language is used to construct and transform the human condition. To illustrate this, I show how the word "genocide" is used in one specific context: Bosnia and Herzegovina.

What Is Rhetoric?

Rhetoric. "Rhetoric" is not a word most middle school English classrooms use when teaching reading or literature, although I have met a few middle school composition teachers who indeed introduce students to the rhetorical triangle (i.e., ethos, pathos, and logos) as part of the writing process. Rhetoric, as understood in most high school English classrooms, is primarily a set of strategies to make arguments more effective, and the word "rhetoric" often implies persuasive communication or even deceit (especially when used in the media to characterize political discourse). When it comes to reading in the English classroom, however, practices that focus strictly on the central message or an objective summary tend to veil the rhetorical nature of a text because its purpose is to achieve a "right" reading. To teach reading without attending to rhetoricality is unethical in that it overlooks the original purpose of that text and the way that text is now being appropriated for a decidedly different purpose (in the classroom). In both cases, the text is attempting to modify or transform a person's perspective, but the implications are quite different.

Any consideration of rhetoric includes an author's intention and the way her message is shaped and received by an audience. Texts, meaning print in addition to images, film, and social media, assume a rhetorical situation, which basically refers to any set of circumstances in which *someone* is using *some form* of communication to modify or transform the perspective of another (i.e., audience). The set of circumstances should be the focus of reading so that students can recognize how *someone* is attempting to modify their perspective or move them to act. Every reader is always already involved rhetorically, and our work in the English classroom is perpetuating a community consciousness of that.

Beyond a simplistic understanding of rhetoric as the persuasive qualities of speech or as a set of techniques used to manipulate others regardless of ethical concerns, rhetoric is about the human condition, meaning the way in which people come to view themselves in relation to others and the world. According to Burke, rhetoric is how people *identify* with one another—how people encourage one another to understand things from one another's perspectives. Understood in this way, rhetoric is not the study of one particular address but a "general *body of identifications* that owe their convincingness much more to trivial repetition and dull daily re-enforcement than to exceptional rhetorical skill" (Burke's emphasis 26). In other words, rhetoric includes how people align themselves with certain interests or groups as the result of repeated, mundane, and usually unremarkable communicative actions. In my view, rhetorical consideration in reading pedagogy illuminates perspectives, interests, and motives, for, as Burke explains,

> however, "pure" one's motives may be actually, the impurities of identification lurking about the edges of such situations introduce a typical Rhetorical wrangle of sort that can never be settled once and for all, but belongs in the field of moral controversy.
>
> (26)

Genocide is an extreme example, but it offers us an example for how notions of identity produce conditions of inclusion and exclusion and ultimately moral controversy. For Burke, rhetoric deals with classification and considers how individuals are at odds with one another. And when language is used to name this group Hutu and that group Tutsi, for example, people become identified with groups that are at odds with one another (22). For Burke, then, there can be no identification without division, identification's "ironic counterpart," and division in the hands (and tongues) of skilled rhetors can bring human beings to commit "millions of cooperative acts" of the most tragic kind (22–23).

Burke explores rhetoric as *beyond* a set of strategies, techniques, or elocutionary options, and I am suggesting that this be our approach to teaching rhetoric in the modern English classroom. Nienkamp explains that rhetoric was generally understood as persuasive speaking and writing but that it can be understood as "a concern with how language in all of its manifestations influences humans (and sometimes other sentient beings)" (3). To consider "language in all its manifestations" means to recognize the rhetoric of progress. In the name of progress, schools have constrained reading practices, and in the name of progress, other institutions have created environmental waste, economic collapse, climate change, war, and genocide. The perspective that progress is always good has hidden the consequences or the darker side of progress. I invoke the term "rhetoricality" to recognize all the conditions of the modern world, to highlight the transactional nature of language, to build in students a capacity for recognizing rhetoricality, and to value rhetoric in the English classroom.

"Rhetoricality" is "rhetoric" plus the affix "ality," which indicates "having the properties of." Rhetoricality is an expanded view of rhetoric as an inherent feature of language or as a condition of our existences as language-using creatures. The term was first used by Bender and Wellbery in 1990. Rhetoricality sees language as exceeding thought or a set of techniques and views language (and texts constructed by language) as not real but representations of the real. Jennifer Richards, in *Rhetoric*, suggests within rhetoric, then, there is fiction: "The social fictions we create are inescapable because they are endemic to language itself, which is the only tool we have to comprehend our world" (133). This notion of "social fictions" calls attention to the provisional nature of knowing. Indeed, in the English class any attempt to understand something is dependent on language, which is never quite adequate to the expression of its meaning. To recognize language in this way—as inadequate and even fiction—may be alarming. However, recognizing what language does and does not quite accomplish is the beautiful problem of language when it comes to representing humanity in words. If we look at the English classroom as a conceptual space to parse out this paradox, I think teachers can better support students in engaging in and even confronting the texts that attempt to shape their understanding of themselves and the world.

In urging English teachers to consider the rhetoricality of texts, I do not mean to suggest that the traditions of rhetoric do not have a place in the modern English classroom. In other words, while I do not object to traditional rhetoric, I see considerations of rhetoricality as preserving and expanding people's subjectivity. In *Rethinking the Rhetorical Tradition*, James Kastely suggests that when we shift from rhetoric as the art of an agent to rhetoricality as a feature of discourse in general, "the issues of justice and responsibility emerge as problems: can the world still be conceived as a scene for action once subjectivity is pluralized and diffused?" (222). Rhetoricality, then, in my view and that of Kastely, is a new rhetoric that "can use the classical tradition and its skeptical challengers as resources for discovery of the possibility for action within a world constituted, in part, by and through rhetoricality" (222). I like this idea of a "skeptical challenger" because skepticism is vital for an individual to understand herself as a subject with agency and responsibility. As a member of society who identifies with certain groups, and as a member who is addressed by rhetors (e.g., state leaders, politicians, reporters, novelists, filmmakers, photographers), we have a responsibility to recognize how our cooperation with certain ideals contributes to both unity and division (Burke). Acts of exclusion, oppression, and domination against individuals occur because such action is part of a system in which social groups and their hierarchy are produced and positioned by rhetoricality; it is a social fiction that social groups are not ontologically equal, and yet how language is used can make that fiction very painful. Thus, an awareness of rhetoricality helps us understand how and why social hierarchies are established and maintained in addition to how we are implicated based on with whom and what we identify.

When we think of language working on our students, engaging them in certain ways for certain purposes, we can see that subjectivity is much more complicated than emotions. In addition to responding as readers to the text in an emotional or aesthetic sense, students must *also* understand themselves as reading rhetorically. Ethical reading depends on students being able to recognize that they are a targeted audience, targeted by writers or speakers with sometimes unethical agendas. And students are also writers who use words to construct their own reality and impress upon others ideas, beliefs, and actions.

The Rhetoric of a Word: "Genocide"

Genocide illuminates this concept of rhetoricality because the word "genocide" was created to name the ideology and systems that excluded certain groups of people in the most extreme example of social injustice. The inquiry that follows considers how the word "genocide" is used across contexts by various rhetors to construct certain ways of understanding genocide and to produce seemingly contrary actions. The naming of genocide after the Holocaust assigned a sound, a word to represent that which is unspeakable; the naming, then, has made it possible to talk about genocide and to use the word to represent certain experiences. However, I hope to show that the English classroom has to go beyond language as communication or as a means to transfer information; if rhetoricality is our condition, then our work must account for how every speaker, utterance, and situation that came before and after are transacting to represent not only a condition of human experience but actions that perpetuate disparate conditions. To be clear, what I see as the benefit of teaching students to understand the rhetoricality of objects, events, and people is that rhetoricality highlights the vast number and type of actions involved in the social construction of the world and our understanding of it. The text is social action. The reading of the text is social action. How the reader responds to the text is social action. And how a community of readers responds to each other's response and makes sense of the text's construction, purpose, and meaning is social action.

On August 24, 1941, in a broadcast to the world, Winston Churchill announced, "We are in the presence of a crime without a name" (British Library of Information). A few years later, this crime was named. In 1944, "genocide" and its definition were constructed by Raphael Lemkin, a Polish Jew and a lawyer who saw genocide as a legal issue. He came to the U.S. during Nazi occupation of Poland, but many of his family members stayed behind and were killed in the Holocaust. Lemkin assisted in drafting the United Nation's "Convention on the Prevention and Punishment of the Crime of Genocide" formally presented on December 9, 1948, and ratified in 1951. According to "The Convention,"

> Genocide is any of the following acts committed with intent to destroy, in whole or in part, a national, ethnical, racial or religious group: (a) killing members of the group; (b) causing serious bodily or mental harm to members of the group; (c) deliberately inflicting on the group conditions of life calculated to bring about its physical destruction in whole or in part; (d) imposing measures intended to prevent births within the group; and (e) forcibly transferring children of the group to another group.

As we can see, the language is quite scientific in that it describes and marks that which will require action or "preparation for" action.

Lemkin crafted this language of genocide carefully so that acts of genocide are identifiable, but language is also a symbol of representation, and here it represents both a history and a future, that which existed and that which is imagined to be. The language names atrocities and appropriates historical imagery for future political, economic, and social action. The sort of action Lemkin imagined this language would bring was action that prevents and punishes crimes against humanity. However, it has failed to do so as evidenced by post-Convention genocides (e.g., Cambodia, Guatemala, Bosnia, Rwanda, Sudan, and more not named here).

Looking at the case of Bosnia and Herzegovina (formerly Yugoslavia), I intend to show how the word "genocide" is actually doing some paradoxical rhetorical work. Indeed, genocide has an ancient past, but in this modern era of projects to improve the human condition, the word "genocide" becomes quite compatible with modernity. We will see in the example that follows what Walter Mignolo has identified as "the darker side of modernity," a side that fails to improve conditions for all humans because only certain individuals are recognized as human by the state. As Bakhtin writes in *The Dialogic Imagination*, "at any given time, in any given place, there will be a set of conditions—social, historical, meteorological, physiological—that will insure that a word uttered in that place and at that time will have a different meaning than it would have under any other conditions" (428). Therefore, my inquiry and the inquiry I suggest English teachers can facilitate with students is this: How is the word "genocide," a word laced with history, making a modernist rhetorical move? To put it another way, the paradox of the word "genocide" is that it actually functions as part of a project of classification and control for opposing purposes, ways that Lemkin could not have imagined.

An utterance like "genocide" becomes definable precisely in terms of certain kinds of actions. In one sense, it is scientific in its careful descriptions. In another sense, the term implies that another kind of action should take place: an action that prevents the previously delineated forms of horrific action. In this second sense, therefore, "genocide" may be said to be rhetorical in that it seeks to persuade people to take the actions necessary to prevent mass killing. However, knowing that oppositional forces are at work, we must ask how the word "genocide" has been used rhetorically when two or more bodies participate in the social discourse and act for different political, cultural, and ideological centralization. How is the word bringing people together or building community? How is the word breaking communities apart?

The word "genocide," as we will see in Bosnia and Herzegovina (formerly Yugoslavia), reveals the darker side of reform, which is the product of order and the effects of naming. In this case, two or more groups of people silencing the "geno" (family, tribe, or race) of "genocide" according to what Bakhtin writes is the " set of conditions . . . that will insure that a word uttered in that place and at that time will have a different meaning than it would have under any other conditions" (428). We will see how "genocide" brings people together for different purposes yet with somewhat similar and troubling results.

Silencing the "Geno" in Bosnia and Herzegovina

Language is a social force that cannot be silenced. It works to move people as an utterance and as an artifact. Bette Denich, a research fellow at Boston University whose work centers on the manipulation of collective memory and public discourse in the formation of ethnic violence, explains the memory of World War II's ethnic conflict in Yugoslavia was deliberately minimized by the Tito regime in the decades that followed. In "Dismembering Yugoslavia," she argues Tito's regime functioned as part of a centralizing force to suppress symbolic reminders of Yugoslavia's ethnic differences for the purpose of creating a new, unified nation state. For example, a play called *The Pigeon Cave* was banned because it restated the massacre of the Serbs and was understood to promote Serbian nationalism. However, and this is the consequence of attempting to silence the "geno," such reminders were later revived to, in fact, dismember Yugoslavia in the late 1980s. The point, in this case, is that modernist classifications of ethnicity functioned to make ethnic divisions "legible" in such a way that they could be managed by a homogenizing power like Tito and to exacerbate ethnic tensions to subvert homogenization. The "geno" of "genocide," however, resists attempts at homogenization; it cannot be silenced.

In discussing the exploitation of historical traumas, Samuel Totten, Professor Emeritus in Curriculum and Instruction at the University of Kansas and scholar of Holocaust and genocide education, explains the historical context by which Slobodan Milosevic, a Serb nationalist, appropriated genocide.

In 1941, three factions emerged within Yugoslavia: the Chetniks, Serbian nationalists who fought against Germans and Italians; Communist Partisans, a multiethnic faction against the Axis forces led by Tito; and the Croatian "Ustasha" led by Ante Pavelić, which was allied with Hitler. Totten writes in *Century of Genocide: Critical Essays and Eyewitness Accounts*, "Between 1941 and 1945, more than 180,000 Serbs were deported, approximately 250,000 forcibly converted to Catholicism from Orthodox Christian faiths, and more than 300,000 murdered" (422). The Communist Partisans won leadership in Yugoslavia and chose to order the state through a homogenizing mechanism of silencing ethnic symbols of genocide. Therefore, the method of ordering postwar Yugoslavia was to eradicate ethnic symbols.

During the Tito regime, survivors of the World War II massacres had to quietly remember the dead by visiting pigeon caves and other unmarked burial sites. The Tito regime did not want to commemorate the burial sites because it did not want reminders of the nationalist ideologies of World War II. Not long after the suppression of the performance of *The Pigeon Cave*, a play that critiques the Ustasha massacre, an outburst of art, literature, and scholarship on national themes portraying Serbian history and the context of the World War II genocide emerged. The author of *The Pigeon Cave*, Jovan Radulovic, set the play in the early 1960s, fifteen years after the end of the war, at a deep cave called Golubnjaca, or "the pigeon cave." During the war, the Ustasha massacred a Serbian village and disposed of their bodies in this cave. Radulovic's protagonists are children; they play war games at the entrance of this cave using the discourse of nationalist ideology they've heard at home. One boy, however, is a war orphan who finds a grenade at the cave; critics argued that the grenade symbolized genocide and the potential of history to destroy this younger generation of Yugoslavs. Because of its political message, this play was banned by Yugoslav party officials in the Tito regime afraid that the contents would incite nationalistic hatred.

In opposition to the homogenizing effort of Tito's regime, the Serbian nationalist revitalization appropriated the "geno" of "genocide" for their cause: to secede from Yugoslavia as its own state. Both Serbs and Croats turned to formulations of nationhood such as the excision of ethnic groups from territory, and, thus, resurrected a framework that had culminated in the pigeon caves, the Ustasha massacres of Serbs by Croats in 1941: genocide.

In this case, we see how genocide is used to argue for a homogenous state for both sides. Denich explains this logic of separation for better relations: "In order to avoid in the future the great suffering the Serbs' neighbors will inflict upon them whenever they have an opportunity to do so, the Chetniks [Serbs] proposed a 'homogenous Serbia'" (375). The friction of ethnic division ultimately led to violence.

On July 25, 1990, the new government of Croatia took office as a real action of division and ethnic opposition. The Ustasha flag was raised, symbolically excluding non-Croats. Serbs knew the coat-of-arms symbol represented the very Croatian nationalism that fueled the massacre of Serbs years ago. Denich argues that "the reappearance of the symbols associated with genocide must be examined in light of memories that had been both individually and collectively repressed and, in light of their transformation, over a half-century, into a cultural artifact of a particular sort" (381). Vuk Draskovic, a Serbian novelist, wrote,

> If war comes, I fear most for the fate of the Croatian people. In Bosnia-Herzegovina and Croatia there isn't a Serb to whom the Croats don't owe several liters of blood. There isn't a house in which someone wasn't massacred. . . . So I understand why Serbs, if war comes, would like to fight against the Croats.
>
> (qtd. in Denich)

Denich clarifies that the *modern* Serbs had not experienced the Ustasha genocide, and "their wartime suffering had come at the hands of the Germans . . . rather than Croats"; however, the pigeon caves were exhumed literally and figuratively for both modern Serbs and Croats to resurrect the narratives of genocide from their ancestors for their own nationalist agenda, a social, political, cultural, and economic agenda.

The state's failure in the Balkans perpetuated conditions for the appropriation of the word "genocide" to rationalize and justify acts of genocide. The language of identification is used rhetorically by all sides in this case for similar albeit divisive purposes. In a sense, there is unity in the way that human beings seek integration by identifying with some and thus against others. Rhetoricality encourages us, alongside our students, to confront the implications of division, and "genocide" certainly illustrates the most tragic, destructive consequences of division.

Beyond the Classroom: Sarajevo

The best reason I had for going to Bosnia and Herzegovina in 2013 is the same reason Philip Gourevitch gives for going to Rwanda in *We Wish to Inform You That Tomorrow We Will Be Killed With Our Families: Stories From Rwanda*: "I am uncomfortable about existence and my place in it" (19). I wanted an excuse to look more closely at "genocide" beyond the classroom, beyond the books that tried to contain the stories. I had been teaching about genocide for several years. I wanted to see what "genocide" meant today for the parents raising their children in a postgenocide state (not that genocide ever ends), for the waiter waiting on tables in a Sarajevan restaurant, for the children going to school with no firsthand knowledge of the genocide.

Because rhetoricality calls attention to the rhetorical view of language as *not real* but *representations of the real*, it was important for me to go beyond the classroom to engage with real people, face to face, an important dimension of rhetoricality but also of education. There is a "real" that language attempts to represent, and I think that, as teachers, we have to help our students reach out to other people in an effort to confront (physically rather than textually) the implications of division when possible. Beyond the texts and beyond the classroom are real human beings who remind us that we can all identify with humankind.

In October 2013, my excuse to look more closely at Bosnia and Herzegovina was a conference. I prepared to attend the annual conference of the Alliance of Universities for Democracy in Sarajevo, Bosnia and Herzegovina. Founded in 1990, the Alliance of American and European universities shares the common purpose of supporting higher learning institutions in their development of democratic development. This year, specifically, members contributed to concerns in southeastern Europe as states engage in democratic nation building and seek peace with justice. Scholars from Bosnia and Herzegovina specifically addressed the fall of Yugoslavia, the Hague Tribunal, responding to the needs of rape survivors during the war, and children's exposure to family violence postwar as an effect of posttraumatic stress disorder.

On the third day of the conference, I met Hasan Nuhanović. Nuhanović is a Bosnian Muslim survivor of the 1995 Srebrenica genocide. From 1992 to 1995, he and his family stayed in the "safe area" protected by the United Nations. Nuhanović became an interpreter for the Dutch, and when Srebrenica fell to the Bosnian Serb Army, Nuhanović's family—his father, mother, and brother—along with five thousand to six thousand refugees found shelter on the U.N. base in Potočari, with some thirty thousand Bosnian Muslims outside the base. "Negotiations" between the U.N. and the Bosnian Serb Army prompted the Dutch to order all refugees out of the base, essentially handing over the refugees to the Serbs because of the humanitarian crises on the U.N. bases, explained in detail in Nuhanović's book *Under the UN Flag: The International Community and the Srebrenica Genocide.* Nuhanović understood the implications of this evacuation and beseeched the Dutch to allow his family to stay with him on the base. Nevertheless, Nuhanović had to interpret the orders and tell his people, including his family, to walk into the hands of the Serbs.

More than eight thousand Bosnian Muslims were killed in and around Srebrenica in July 1995. In 2008, the remains of Nuhanović's father were discovered in a secondary mass grave, which means there was a reburial effort to conceal evidence of mass murders. In early 2010, his mother's remains were found not far from his family home in Vlasenic. He wrote in an editorial, "The Serbs who lived there threw garbage on her for 14 years. She wasn't alone. They killed another six in the same place. Burned them. I hope they were burned only after they died" ("15 Years After the Srebrenica Massacre"). And then in June 2010, Nuhanović identified his brother by his tennis shoes.

In 2013 Sarajevo, Nuhanović says that Muslims, Croats, and Serbs find a way to survive if not *with* one another then *next* to one another. In a sense they share a story; however, their memories of the past ring of dissonance. Public symbols of genocide, visible and "invisible," blanket the fractured country. Here is what Nuhanović had to say about Sarajevo and its symbols:

> It's an open city. Serbs come here for shopping if they don't live here. There are Serbs living here, of course, but a far fewer number than Bosniaks. The majority of the population in this city is now Bosniaks [Muslims]. Just like the majority of the population in Eastern Bosnia is [Serb]. Just walk across the invisible—it's supposed to be invisible—Inter-Entity Boundary Line . . . but the Serbs made it visible. When you go there, like three miles from here, you will hit the sign saying "Welcome to The Republic of Srpska." If you enter Sarajevo from the other side, it will not say "Welcome to The Federation of Bosnia and Herzegovina." We are not proud, officially, we are not proud of being an entity within Bosnia and Herzegovina, but the Serbs are proud . . . trying, of course, to undermine and emphasize their own statehood within a state. You get the message if you are not a Serb, and I am not a Serb. And I have survived all this, and when I read the sign "Welcome to the Republic of Srpska," what does it mean? *Srpska* means Serb. Is that? What? I am not a Serb, so how am I supposed to feel being in a place that stole Srpska? At least the federation does not bear the name of any ethnicity . . . even though Serbs refer to it as the Muslim-Croat Federation.
>
> (AUDEM address)

The rhetorical situation was clear to me as I listened to Nuhanović. Here we were in an international conference on democracy listening to Nuhanović remember and account for what happened to him and his family. He represented it in such a way as to communicate clearly to his audience that by most accounts, the past is not forgotten. The past cannot be forgotten because this Inter-Entity Boundary Line is, in fact, not invisible. The peace treaty did not resolve the conflict, and the genocide has not ended. He was, for us, witnessing the genocide of his family all over again for us so that we would see the symbolic representations of genocide that exist throughout the country. The language on the signs and the state-created boundary line are making different claims about what happened. How one interprets that boundary, as achieving peace or maintaining an exclusionary system, depends on a multitude of transactions, but Nuhanović wanted to be sure that he had some influence over how we understood Srebrenica and Bosnia and Herzegovina and how we will tell the story of Srebrenica to others.

In old town Sarajevo, teens smoke cigarettes and shop in designer clothing stores, unaware of what the symbols represent to Nuhanović's generation. Schools do not teach about the Siege of Sarajevo or the genocide in Srebrenica because the case of genocide is ongoing. As recent as July 2014, a Dutch court ruled that the Netherlands government is liable for the deaths of about three hundred victims in the 1995 Srebrenica massacre in Bosnia, saying that the United Nations' Dutch peacekeepers failed to prevent those deaths. Efforts to exhume the remains of those killed in the genocide to identify victims and perpetrators are unsettling any sense of reconciliation between Muslims and Serbs. Even though there is a museum to tell the story of Srebrenica in the heart of Sarajevo, it is more for the tourists (like me) than for the people of Sarajevo. Many Sarajevans are ready for Bosnia and Herzegovina to represent something other than genocide (like their soccer team, their cuisine, their architecture). It seems that while some want to quiet the past and make invisible symbols of ethnic tension, others want to exhume the past and make visible symbols of hate.

To some parts of the world, Sarajevo represents solidarity when during the Siege of Sarajevo, citizens cut off from food, water, electricity, and first aid supplies built an underground tunnel to transport supplies from the safe zone. To other parts of the world, however, Sarajevo represents insufficient peace. The rhetoric of the Dayton Peace Accords, especially when taught in public schools, can be communicated as a solution, as a victory of diplomatic negotiation by and in the West. However, many Bosnians born in Srebrenica have yet to return home now that the road from Sarajevo to Eastern Bosnia is paved with Serbian signs. The reason this conference was in Bosnia and Herzegovina is because while there was a peace agreement signed in 1995, this country is still a divided country with a pervasive if hushed ethnic tension that may prevent Bosnia and Herzegovina from ever joining the European Union. People from all over the world interested in democracy and education flew into Sarajevo over one weekend in mid-October to understand this tension and to talk about what education can do to support peace and equality for everyone.

My last night in Sarajevo, it was raining. My husband and I grabbed our umbrella and began a half-hour walk into the hills for dinner at *4 Sobe Gospodje Safije*, The Four Rooms of Mrs. Safije. This 1910 building commemorates the tale of a forbidden love affair between Safije, a Sarajevan girl, and Johan, an Austrian count, during the city's shift from Turkish to Austro-Hungarian rule. Modern designers have updated the interior while leaving the four-room structure intact. At the end of our meal, our waiter asked us where we were from. "Chicago," we answered. He then told us he had a sister in Minnesota but had no intention of leaving Sarajevo. "It is my home," he told us.

As we put on our coats and headed for the door, we discovered our umbrella had been taken, and as he found another umbrella for us to take on our walk back to our hotel, we thanked him. He replied, "And thank you for not asking me about the war."

As Bakhtin writes, "a word uttered in that place and at that time will have a different meaning than it would have under any other conditions" (428). The word, the place, the time, the conditions, and those uttering the word or silencing the word shape its meaning, but as we have also seen here, an utterance leads to actions that have consequences extending to other times and places. On that rainy night in Sarajevo, I did not utter the word, but the waiter recognized its silence.

Conclusion

Given the degree to which genocide has permeated the international community and the sheer number of people murdered by state violence since the Holocaust, why have our schools given so little attention to rhetoricality and the discourses that shape our understanding of international issues and how nation states are not only politically and economically but ethically implicated in human rights violations? We don't want another generation to be ignorant of the globalized nature of our world nor think they are immune to the social forces that shape our political, economic, and social systems. One of those social forces is language. Our discipline, English, in public schools has been complicit in perpetuating a narrow understanding of language when we can be doing so much more.

The distance between skills-based instruction and teaching students to understand that "racial, national, ethnic, and religious hatred can lead to horrible tragedies" is vast and as such exposes a deeper problem of literacy education, one with ethical implications for what we teach (or don't) and how we teach in our increasingly globalized world. I think what and how we teach has everything to do with how we, as teachers, not only interpret state mandates but read the world and understand the role of English in preparing students to also read the world, as I illustrated with the word "genocide" here. The standards do emphasize rhetorical analysis, argumentation, inquiry, evidence, and primary sources such as testimony. However, the new standards do not address core issues of democracy and humanity: rights, oppression, power, discrimination, and nonviolence. The new standards do not advise how teachers are to implement the standards in their content areas, and so now is the time for our profession to resist packaged curriculum and engage with the words that construct our world. Middle and secondary English classrooms can be sites where teachers and students, through conscious reading practices, illuminate and counteract the ways standards and high-stakes tests constrain the way we read and think about reading, limit our purposes for reading literature, narrow the goal of education, and impede discussions of our responsibility as members of an increasingly globalized society.

Works Cited

Bakhtin, Mikhail. *The Dialogic Imagination: Four Essays*. Austin: University of Texas Press, 1981. Print.

Bender, John. *Ends of Enlightenment*. Stanford University Press, 2012. Print.

Bender, John, and David E. Wellbery. *The Ends of Rhetoric: History, Theory, Practice*. Stanford: Stanford University Press, 1990. Print.

Burke, Kenneth. *A Rhetoric of Motives*. New York: Prentice-Hall, 1952. Print.

Churchill, Winston. "Prime Minister Winston Churchill's Broadcast to the World About the Meeting with President Roosevelt." *British Library of Information*. 24 Aug. 1941. Web.

"The Convention on the Prevention and Punishment of the Crime of Genocide." *Prevent Genocide International*. 22 Apr. 2011. Web.

Denich, Bettie. "Dismembering Yugoslavia: Nationalist Ideologies and the Symbolic Revival of Genocide." *American Ethnologist*. 21.2: 367-390. (Apr. 1994): 367–390. Web.

Gourevitch, Philip. *We Wish to Inform You That Tomorrow We Will Be Killed With Our Families: Stories from Rwanda*. New York: Farrar, Straus, and Giroux, 1998. Print.

Kastely, James L. *Rethinking the Rhetorical Tradition: From Plato to Postmodernism*. New Haven, CT: Yale University Press, 1997. Print.

Mignolo, Walter D. *The Darker Side of Western Modernity: Global Futures, Decolonial Options*. Durham, NC: Duke University Press, 2011. Print.

Moss, Mallory. "The Language of Genocide." *The Hill*. 24 Apr. 2014. Web.

Nienkamp, Jean. *Internal Rhetorics: Toward a History and Theory of Self-Persuasion*. Carbondale: Southern Illinois University Press, 2001. Print.

Nuhanović, Hasan. "15 Years After the Srebrenica Massacre, a Survivor Buries His Family." *The Washington Post.com*. 11 July. 2010. Web.

———. "Srebrenica Memorial." AUDEM, Sarajevo University. Sarajevo, Bosnia Herzegovina. 12 Oct. 2013. Keynote Address.

———. *Under the UN Flag: The International Community and the Srebrenica Genocide*. Sarajevo: DES, 2007. Print.

Radulovic, Jovan. *The Pigeon Cave and Other Stories*. Belgrade: Rad, 1989. Print.

Richards, Jennifer. *Rhetoric*. New York: Routledge, 2008. Print.

Totten, Samuel, and William Parsons. *Century of Genocide: Essays and Eyewitness Accounts*. New York: Routledge, 2012. Print.

Literature for Your Classroom Library

Filipović, Zlata. *Zlata's Diary: A Child's Life in Sarajevo*. New York: Viking, 1994. Print.

Galloway, Steven. *The Cellist of Sarajevo*. New York: Riverhead Books, 2008. Print.

Halilbegovićh, Nadja. *My Childhood Under Fire: A Sarajevo Diary*. Toronto: Kids Can Press, 2006. Print.

Heleta, Savo. *Not My Turn to Die: Memoirs of a Broken Childhood in Bosnia*. New York: AMACOM, 2008. Internet resource.

Mead, Alice. *Girl of Kosovo*. New York: Farrar Straus Giroux, 2001. Print.

Ross, Stewart. *Only a Matter of Time: A Story from Kosovo*. London: Hodder Wayland, 2001. Print.

4 Reading Testimony

Witnessing and the Witness

Mandates and standards position teachers as responsible for meeting those requirements. However, mandates and standards rarely say how a teacher should teach or why. In the case of the genocide mandate, we know that the purpose is to (1) recognize that crimes against humanity continue to be perpetrated across the globe and (2) deter indifference to such crimes and human suffering wherever they may occur. However, no unit of instruction, especially if it is ancillary and limited to stage identification, can bring about the sort of change we need to stop crimes against humanity at home and across the globe. Rhetoric is one way English teachers can illuminate how words create conditions that sustain frameworks of inclusion and exclusion, how institutions work to legitimize certain groups and knowledge. To intervene in the exclusionary conditions I've noted in schools and states, teachers and students have to see themselves as witnesses to both the systems that create inequality and the people the systems impact. From the stance of a witness, we learn to attend to others and the systems that impact them. In recognizing others, we begin to feel a call to better understand the systems that create injustice and to, ultimately, intervene. The teacher's job, then, is to prepare students to listen, read, and respond to stories of humanity in ethical ways so as not to perpetuate unjust systems.

In this chapter, I suggest that, in addition to recognizing rhetoricality, the English classroom must nurture and support an ethical practice of *witnessing*, a practice that cultivates an engagement with the people constructing the text (film or image) and represented in the text as an active way of considering our epistemological and ethical responsibility to people and their causes. Witnessing is a *principled basis* for reading and listening to stories told by other human beings. It is neither autonomous nor authoritative but a deliberative stance that acknowledges we need others to make sense of our shared world. This kind of witnessing is facilitated by transactional readings and rhetorical analyses. The genre that best teaches us how to witness each other's lives is testimonial literature because it asks that we attend to the testifier *and* how she is able to tell her story. Such literature is an opportunity to practice a rhetorical analysis that considers how a text mediates our perception. Thus, we will continue our study of genocide and how to teach it. I will focus on the genre of genocide testimonial literature because, in my experience, it can help us become proper witnesses of people who enable us to make sense of our shared world and prompt us to action.

What's Wrong With Feeling Sorry for the Victim?

In *Spectacular Rhetorics*, Wendy Hesford, scholar of rhetorical theory, human rights, and law and literature, explains that discourses about human rights tend to transform the focus on human rights into a spectacle that positions some nations as more powerful or ethical. In other words, whereas the attention should be *on the situation* that caused a human rights violation (land disputes, political power, resources) and *on the people* violated, the focus shifts to the feelings or ideas *of the person or institution* learning about or reacting to the violation. As teachers who potentially confront students with stories and images of human rights violations, the question Hesford raises is how we can ethically notice, read, and respond to human rights violations.

In the case of genocide mandates and standards, government, schools, teachers, and even students learning about "violations" in other countries are situated in a position of safety, privilege, and power, most not having experienced the atrocities. If teachers follow the mandate, students read about Armenia, Ukraine, Cambodia, Bosnia, Rwanda, and Sudan; they might respond with sympathy for the victims; they might begin to see how the word "genocide" is used by survivors, perpetrators, and international agencies for opposing causes. Still, though students are engaged emotionally and reading rhetorically, they are far removed from the situation and struggle to understand what to do with their reading experience and knowledge. The problem with students reading about atrocities is that distance—spatial and temporal—obscures a sense of responsibility for how they respond and relate to victims, survivors, and violence. How can we teach reading so that students recognize their agency and responsibility in the interaction with the text? How can we teach teens to ethically carry the stories and ideas they encounter when reading the world?

According to Samera Esmier, in "On Making Dehumanization Possible," because human rights campaigns and various agents of memory tell "what happened" in novels, films, poems, and news reports using images and testimony from victims, we focus on and respond to people "thought to be dehumanized by their regimes and awaiting the promise of humanization by international human rights campaigns and legal reforms" (1546). For Esmier, Hesford, and for me, any account of the scene of an atrocity is a rhetorical address, and the witness (reader, audience) is moved to look for a way of relating to the dehumanized victim. Any depiction of *de*humanization, however, invites us (and even conditions us) to see the people we are reading about as without humanity; by not providing identification other than that of *victim*, humanity becomes a matter of "endowment, declaration, or recognition," and we as reader-witnesses become the endowers (1549). Because the reader-witness is positioned to look at the spectacle of suffering and feel pity for the victim rather than to contemplate her responsibility as a witness, the *learning about* "victims" can reproduce hierarchies of race, nation, and class even if the intention is to bring about awareness and change. To be clear, then, I am suggesting that when we read about genocide in the English classroom, even if we are responding emotionally and recognizing rhetoricality, we can potentially perpetuate systems of oppression and exploitation by failing to recognize and acknowledge the full humanity of the victims.

To respond to how we *ought* to read, Hesford suggests that beyond seeking some understanding of suffering or some shared, felt experience, we *ought to* consider how human rights representations constitute the witnessing publics they seek to engage, specifically by acknowledging our perception as a mediated act. Rather than consumers of information about genocide, we can consider ourselves as global witnesses. Witnessing implies ethical responsibility. "Witnessing," according to Carrie Rentschler, "is a rhetorical act constituted by multiple levels of mediation: material artifacts, media texts, bodies, aesthetics, cultural and national politics, and so on" (298). Human rights media (news, public service announcements, social media, reports, essays, films, books) make audiences global witnesses to historical events and human suffering to build awareness and perhaps to fulfill the promise of "never again"; however, Rentschler warns that "witnesses can also act complicitously in others' suffering by watching it without seeking to alleviate it" (298). What Rentschler names a witness, however, Hesford names a spectator. Hesford suggests that the danger in seeking any "imaginative identification with the suffering other" is that we become complicit in "transforming the other into an object of feeling and sight" (57). In this case, the reader or viewer is more of a *spectator*, captivated by the spectacle of human suffering, than a *witness*. Witnessing, I will show, constitutes an obligation to attend in a way that spectatorship does not.

If we think of witnessing's rhetorical dimensions, we become conscious of *how* media (texts, images, films) align audiences with the suffering other, regimes, institutions, and other media. For Hesford—and in my view—our work as witnesses to global atrocities is to consider "how these rhetorical alignments as scenes of address foster certain forms of recognition, engagement, and action" (57). For me, if English teachers can begin a rhetorical analysis of the *how*, as in how texts mediate our perception, we might transform how our students recognize, engage, and act with other human beings beyond the walls of the classroom. The rhetoric of genocide illuminates the importance of teaching English in ways that build consciousness of the human beings who are using language (and images) for sometimes opposing causes. Students must learn habits of reading and seeing that help them recognize how they are being drawn into the spectacle of distant suffering as spectators and positioned in a hierarchy of humanity in the hopes that they can be more than spectators in this world. Witnessing in a time of standards and accountability teaches students to go beyond the role of spectator in their world, to practice how they might engage with distant human beings to create a more just society.

In the next section, I will define testimonial literature as a genre written by firsthand witnesses to atrocities. I offer this chapter to demonstrate how teachers might approach a text written by a genocide survivor to read as a witness rather than as a spectator.

What Is Testimonial Literature?

As readers, we are witnesses to stories told by others, questions we did not know to ask, and discoveries that are not ours. But when we read the testimony of a genocide witness, we become that survivor's listener and bear witness to her testimony. According to Shoshana Felman in *Testimony* (Felman and Laub), when a survivor of genocide (or other human rights violations) feels impelled to transmit her testimony, the testimony is *addressed* to others and invites transactions. For Felman, the witness-reader is the vehicle of an occurrence "composed of bits and pieces of a memory that has been overwhelmed by occurrences that have not settled into understanding or remembrance, acts that cannot be constructed as knowledge nor assimilated into full cognition" (5). In other words, testimony is not a "totalizable account" of those events (2). Witnesses have dealt with their memory of genocide experiences in a variety of literary forms that can be considered "art": testimonial narrative, extended essays, novels, short stories, and poetry. My focus in this chapter is on testimonial literature: testimony that is a written, published, first-person, autobiographical narrative in literary idiom, though I believe my argument extends to other literary forms. In *Holocaust Testimonies*, Lawrence Langer writes:

> Written memoirs, by the very strategies available to their authors—style, chronology, analogy, imagery, dialogue, a sense of character, a coherent moral vision—strive to narrow this space [the space of imagination separating what the victim has endured from the reader's capacity to understand it], easing us into their unfamiliar world through familiar (and hence comforting?) literary devices.
>
> (19)

Written memoirs, then, involve conscious choices in language to transform memory into a coherent and sharable narrative. The medium, then, acknowledges gaps between the experience of the events and efforts to assign language to that experience.

Autobiographies and memoirs are literary representations of their authors' life histories, yet the question of how to represent one's life and how to account for what she witnessed offers writers and readers challenges unique to this genre. What the witness-writer owes to the reader is the ability to persuade her that the narrator is *trying* to represent the experience at hand.

It is a "given that memory isn't factual or accurate, nor should anyone claim it to be"; it is an expression of "a series of fragments, moments, memories, dreams, perceptions, lies and stabs at truth" (Lauck). The witness-writer is impelled to revisit her trauma and share it with the public. Elie Wiesel, a Holocaust memoirist, said he penned his memories of living in concentration camps "to justify my own survival" (1995, 2); "I needed to give some meaning to my survival" (2006, viii). Wiesel, and other testimonial writers, enters a relationship with language, depending on language to help him establish an account of his experience. James Young, in *Writing and Rewriting the Holocaust*, interprets testimony and suggests: "Even if narrative cannot document events, or constitute perfect factuality, it can document the actuality of the writer and text. The writer and link to events may thus be reified not in the writer's words, but in the writing activity that brought words to the page" (420). In other words, understanding testimonial literature means recognizing that a real person somehow needed to tell her story and that the writing of the story was instrumental in remembering her experiences. The words on the page do not (cannot) tell the whole story of the event, of the writer, or of the meaning to her survival, but because someone (our students) will read those words, the writer might "justify" her survival.

Testimonial literature is specific to the author; it cannot give the wider picture or list chronological stages, but what it does is to depict and scrutinize the effect upon individuals of the events taking place, even when those events are not fully understood by the narrators. Judith Kelly wrote about the human and historical value of Primo Levi's testimonial literature *If This Is a Man*. The value, she argues,

> resides not in its documentary accuracy, not in any reliance upon dates, figures and facts, but in its personal, subjective nature, its recounting of the experience of the individual, and, in so doing, its reconstruction of that experience in such a way that the reader—any reader, at any time—can come to some understanding of it.
>
> (2)

Testimonial literature, then, is a genre in need of an informed and ethical readership, informed in understanding the genre but, perhaps more importantly, ethical in the practice of reading testimonial literature.

The Reader as a Witness

Witnessing considers the relation between literature and testimony, between the writer and the witness. In the English classroom, our reading of testimonial literature enables the unfolding of accounts of trauma and genocide. However, the mere reading of genocide literature does not necessarily fulfill a testimonial resolution. For the testimony to emerge, a reader must carry out her responsibilities as a secondhand or belated witness: to understand the emergence of the narrative and how she is positioned by the narrative to observe, remember, and carry on the testimony. Testimony is a means toward witnessing rather than a means toward some fixed or static knowledge. Witnessing in the English classroom, then, means being conscious of our alignment with and responsibility to the writer of testimony; it is a practice of relating to others in an ethical and responsible way.

Witnessing should be distinguished from other possible responses to testimony such as voyeurism and spectatorship. Voyeurism is the act of obsessively watching others, and spectatorship is the act of watching something without taking part. The principal characteristic of both is that the voyeur or spectator does not interact directly with the subject, which positions the subject as a distant spectacle. In witnessing, however, the testifier recognizes the listener, depends on the listener to witness her testimony. The witness to the testimony comes to "partially experience the trauma in himself" (Felman and Laub 57). In other words, if we think of reading as a way of listening to or witnessing testimony, the reader takes part and, in doing so, becomes implicated in a number of ways. For Simon and Eppert, in "Remembering Obligation: Pedagogy and the Witnessing of Testimony of Historical Trauma," "the first-order witness initiates a chain of testimony held together by the bonds of an ethics forged in relation of responsibility and respect" (176). The reader reads the words of the witness and becomes a witness (secondhand witness), and the reader, through the act of reading, is "placed under the obligation of response to an embodied singular experience not recognizable to one's own" (176). The alignment between the reader-listener and the testifier-witness suggests that reading-as-witnessing obliges the reader to "double attentiveness," an attentiveness to ethical and epistemological responsibilities. Double attentiveness, for Simon and Eppert, is a condition for witnessing testimony that means "attending to what is said while hearing how the saying of testimony undoes the discursive grasp one has of the other's story" (183). To be clear, testimony imposes certain obligations on those who receive it, obliging the reader to take part. How the reader takes part is a question of ethics, that is, how we view ourselves in relation to the subject and what we believe society *ought* to be.

I think that reader response is a necessary foundation to the practice of reading as witnessing because of the emotional response evoked by testimonial literature. The reader must be allowed or rather encouraged to experience the text and must have ample time to respond personally and emotionally before deliberating interpretation with her community of readers. The process of reading testimonial literature is particularly tenuous because the reader is responding to a firsthand account of genocide, an account by a real person. As a reader in the act of reading, the "knowing" of the event is realized, and she becomes party to the creation of knowledge, however unsettled or fragmented. In other words, the reader-listener (secondhand witness) becomes a participant and co-owner of the traumatic event; these two distant beings become aligned (Felman and Laub 57). If the testimony-text is an alignment between the reader-listener and the testifier-witness, what would this alignment mean? What are the implications? The meaning of this alignment is that two people are entering the plane of the text—one who by the definition of genocide should not exist and the other who has the privilege of bearing witness to that experience. The testimony-text is not "real" but a representation of "real"; still, the testifier's words are real, and the reader is real. Texts written by witnesses to atrocities serve as a reminder that our world is divided in zones of safety and danger, wealth and poverty, and progress and stagnation; they raise questions of how such discrepancies persist and what to do.

Witnessing as a stance for reading is a way of attending to practical and moral claims because it is a stance in which readers take responsibility for their role in a reading transaction, a responsibility that recognizes the rhetoricality of the text, specifically how the testifier uses language to represent an event and her experiences to serve a cause. The testifier is first the author of the testimonial literature, but the witness-reader, once without such a memory, becomes an agent of memory who will share and potentially teach others about the author's life. The witness-reader becomes a co-owner of the story and thus responsible for it. The reading does not end with questions at the end of the text or some test. The testimony is forever imprinted in the mind (and heart) of the reader. This perspective of reading contrasts greatly with standards-based learning, which focuses on measurable outcomes.

One way of thinking about a reader's obligation is Simon and Eppert's focus on what to do after reading a testimony. They suggest the secondhand witness ought to carry stories of past injustice "beyond their moment of telling by taking those stories to another time and space where they become available to be heard or seen" by "re-presenting" the story to others, or by enacting "one's relationship with others so as to make evident that one's practice has been informed by the living memory of prior testimony" (178). Their article offers suggestions for class activities where students re-present through words, images, and actions what is "worthy of remembrance" (178). While I agree witnessing obliges the reader to respond ethically, I do not necessarily agree that re-presenting a survivor's testimony is the most ethical response or that readers should feel obliged to attempt a retelling. Testimonial literature is carefully crafted, and I would not presume to decide nor ask my students to decide what is worth remembering from a victim's testimony. However, I do see Simon and Eppert's double attentiveness as an ethical response and act that has been informed by witnessing. Therefore, I offer that reading-as-witnessing is about practicing our attentiveness to intertwined epistemological and ethical responsibilities as readers. Teachers are the guide in this practice, so they must read alongside students.

The witness's obligation to the testifier is to accept epistemological responsibility—to be concerned with *how* knowledge of a given subject could be obtained. How is it possible that this writer of the text (the eyewitness testifying) knows what happened if she was traumatized, for example? To be clear, I am not suggesting that the reader-witness necessarily accuse the testifier of fraudulence; rather, I am suggesting the reader-witness attend to the writing activity that brought the words to the page for her privilege of bearing witness to another person's life. The reader becomes "an apprentice to the provision of memory," which is to say the reader learns, as she listens to the testimony, the limits of what one can say and needs to say and tries to respond to what lies beyond (Simon and Eppert 179). In some cases, there may be intentional deception in testimony, and it is also the responsibility of the modern English classroom to do inquiry into the publication and distribution of testimonial texts. The ethical reader, thus, attends to *how* a person translates her experience of trauma across time and space, which means she has to decipher what the testifier claims to know and what she does not or could not know. In other words, the ethical reader considers the rhetoricality of the text. (See Chapter 9 for a classroom example).

To accept ethical responsibility is to attend to all these epistemological concerns so that the testifier does not have to carry the story alone. The transactions among the testifier, the reader, and the reading process teach the reader the privilege of bearing witness to another life quite distant from their own (Felman and Laub 85) rather than teaching readers to act "complicitously in others' suffering" (Rentschler 298) or view the other as an "object of feeling and sight" (Hesford 57). The privilege of bearing witness, however, is not without some degree of trauma for the reader.

Trauma: The Ethics of Teaching Reading as Witnessing

A reader-as-witness can be seen as a companion, listening to the testifier as she witnesses her own suffering. What does this companion, now aligned to the testifier, do with this new knowledge and experience? Dori Laub, M.D., the co-author of *Testimony*, testimonial interviewer of Holocaust survivors, and child survivor of the Holocaust, examines what it means to bear witness to a testimony. Through his work as an interview-listener, he considers the implications of listening to testimony. For our purposes as English teachers, I'd like to consider how reading, like listening, aligns the testifier-witness and the reader-witness. In this case, we would consider the adolescent reader as the listener to the narrative of human pain. In the teen reader, the testimony to the trauma of the victim is inscribed anew. Unlike the historical documents and artifacts about an event, in the event of reading a testimonial narrative, the "knowing of the event is given birth to" (Laub 57). The listener, our student, comes to be what Laub calls a "co-owner" of the event who, he suggests, partially experiences the event and the trauma. The reader-listener, then, must attend to the feelings that the victim experiences if the trauma is to emerge and for witnessing to take place. At this point, many teachers might be thinking that it is unethical to ask a teenager to carry such a burden. Indeed, it may be, but it also may be that the English classroom can be a place where students and teachers work together to ponder such ethical questions related to literary representation of trauma, where a community of witnesses can address "bewilderment, injury, confusion, dread and conflicts that the trauma victim feels" (58).

Reading testimonial literature has its hazards. How can the child reader assume the testimony and maintain perspective that she is not the victim? In her essay about testimony in her college class, Felman writes:

> [Readers cannot] fulfill their task without, in turn, passing through the crisis of experiencing their boundaries, their separateness, their functionality, and indeed their sanity, at risk. They have to learn how to recognize these hazards, how to integrate these pitfalls of the witnessing into the fulfillment of their . . . human task, and how to bond with the narrator in a common struggle to release the testimony.
>
> (Felman and Laub xvii)

Once the listener engages with testimony in such a way that she shares some aspect of the experience of the original witness, she cannot ignore any number of experiences or questions:

> the question of death, of facing time and its passage; of the meaning and purpose of living; of the limits of one's omnipotence; of losing the ones that are close to us; the great question of our ultimate aloneness; our otherness from any other; our responsibility to and for our destiny; the question of loving and its limits; of parents and children; and so on.
>
> (Felman and Laub 72)

Even in middle school classrooms, testimonial literature can evoke deep philosophical discussions about the power and limitations of language to ask, explore, discover, and sometimes answer questions about humanity. The teacher and students must be aware of potential, protective responses to existential questions explored in testimonial literature. According to Laub, students may withdraw, express outrage, foreclose through facts, becoming obsessed with fact finding to assuage uncertainty, and/or respond hyperemotionally. Hyperemotion, according to Laub, looks like compassion and caring but acts as "defensive affectivity" and can drown out the testifier (Felman and Laub 73). While the defenses may be conscious or unconscious, there is this urgency as reader-listeners to pull back, to distance ourselves from the other's suffering. What can we learn from this sense of urgency, from the trauma of listening, from the testimony, and from the very process of our listening? Is the trauma of witnessing worth the testimony? The answer, I think, is to consider what would be lost had we not read that testimony, had we not experienced urgency, had we not listened, had we not been a witness to that life. In many ways it is a privilege to bear witness, and I think this experience is one that has been marginalized in classrooms in the name of achievement and accountability.

Laub's work (in Felman and Laub) is an important call to teachers to include testimonial literature in our curriculum and to practice reading as witnessing. In Laub's chapter, "An Event without a Witness," he explains how the survivors could not bear witness during the *actual* occurrence. And this seems so fascinating to me and helpful in understanding why we should read testimonial literature, why it is essential to modern education. The survivors did not have the capacity to be aware or to comprehend the event during the occurrence—"its dimensions, consequences, and above all, its radical *otherness* to all known frames of reference" (84). To give and to listen to testimony calls attention to the human will to live and desire to know the "circumstances designed for its obliteration and destruction" (84). What was the totality of the event? What were the beliefs, ideas, and systems that made the event possible? What are the institutions (such as schools) that cultivated the beliefs and ideas? Laub ends his chapter with what is incredibly important in arguing for genocide literature in our schools, for what it can do for human beings and our citizenry:

> It is the realization that the lost ones are not coming back; the realization that what life is all about is precisely living with an unfulfilled hope; only this time with the sense that you are not alone any longer—that someone can be there as your companion—knowing you, living with you through the unfulfilled hope, someone saying, "I'll be with you in the very process of your losing me. I am your witness."
>
> (92)

Reading testimonies is an opportunity to contemplate in their own terms (though prompted by the testimony) essential questions about the human condition. Indeed, bearing witness to trauma can be difficult and risky, and this risk leads some to justify silence as a preferred ethical and pedagogical response, but such a position constrains experiences and knowledge and potentially meaning making. An ethical education teaches the courage to witness. A teacher, who also experiences the trauma of witnessing, can help make reading testimonial literature a productive, human experience.

Testimonies are communicative practices that convey to others a sense of prior events; testimonies of historical trauma attempt to translate the tangibility of occurrences across time and space. As translations they are insufficient and inadequate to render fully the realities of human cruelty and suffering and limited by memory of the past. Testimonies enact betrayal. The betrayed has the obligation to convey "what happened" to those who survived and to those whose deaths ended the possibility of their witness. The rhetoricality of testimony allows the listener to attend to what is said while hearing how the saying undoes the grasp one has of the other's story. According to Levinas, "The unspoken is necessary, so that listening remains a way of thinking" (80). Reading must also remain a way of thinking.

Conclusion

Learning how to witness another's life promotes ethical social action. Felman and Laub's work with testimony and witnessing has illuminated, for me, how I have taught students to read as somewhat passive spectators to trauma and suffering not only with genocide literature but all literature. Much of my reading instruction in the era of NCLB had been focused on accumulating knowledge rather than considering our reading and viewing habits as spectators—disinterested, unimplicated readers. Hesford asks us to go beyond recognition, beyond the spectacle, beyond knowing *about* something to uncover what causes such conditions and how we are implicated. I argue that to do this, we have to, first, read rhetorically to understand the situation and people who are using the words and images to get our attention and, second, to be witnesses rather than spectators in the world. We can begin by testifying to our own lives and listening to the testimony of those with whom we share our days. For most English classes, students spend about forty to fifty minutes a day with the same people, and in most school years, that is for about 180 days. Let's start there as an answer to how we deter indifference to human suffering. In witnessing our own lives and bearing witness to the lives of others, we become conscious of the process of communicating stories of humanity. In Chapter 9, I share a story from my classroom of how we wrote memoirs and read Loung Ung's testimony. This experience profoundly changed the way I teach. However, before we go into the classroom, I will explore how rhetoric and witnessing work with the reading of fiction.

Works Cited

Esmier, Samera. "On Making Dehumanization Possible." *The Humanities in Human Rights: Critique, Language, Politics.* Modern Language Association, 2005. 1544–1551. Print.

Felman, Shoshana, and Dori Laub. *Testimony: Crises of Witnessing in Literature, Psychoanalysis, and History.* New York: Routledge, 1991. Print.

Hesford, Wendy S. *Spectacular Rhetorics: Human Rights Visions, Recognitions, Feminisms.* Durham: Duke University Press, 2011. Print.

Kelly, Judith. *Primo Levi: Recording and Reconstruction in the Testimonial Literature.* Leicester: Troubador Publishing, 2000. Print.

Langer, Lawrence. *Holocaust Testimonies: The Ruins of Memory.* New Haven: Yale University Press, 1991. Print.

Lauck, Jennifer. "The Memoir Dilemma: What's With All These Memoirs?" *Huffingtonpost.com.* 21 Feb. 2011. Web.

Levinas, Emmanuel. *Beyond the Verse: Talmudic Readings and Lectures.* Trans. G. D. Mole. Bloomington: University of Indiana Press, 1994. 68–95. Print.

Rentschler, Carrie. "Witnessing: U.S. Citizenship and the Vicarious Experiences of Suffering." *Media Culture, and Society.* 26.2 (2004): 297–304. Web.

Simon, Roger, and Claudia Eppert. "Pedagogy and the Witnessing Testimony of Historical Trauma." *Canadian Journal of Education.* 22.2 (1997): 175–191. Web.

Wiesel, Elie. *Night.* New York: Hill and Wang, 2006. Print.

Young, James E. *Writing and Rewriting the Holocaust: Narrative and the Consequences of Interpretation.* Bloomington: Indiana University Press, 1988. Print.

Part III

Rhetorical Appeals in Fiction

5 The Rhetoric and Aesthetic of Fiction in Genocide Literature

> The novel constructs a paradigm of a style of ethical reasoning that is context-specific without being relativistic, in which we get potentially universalizable concrete prescriptions by bringing a general idea of human flourishing to bear on a concrete situation which we are invited to enter through imagination.
>
> —Martha Nussbaum, *Poetic Justice*

Ten years after the genocide mandate, I teach in the very classroom where I identified "bubble kids": H103 (Chapter 1). Diane and Elaine have retired, and new teachers have joined Lincoln's faculty. No Child Left Behind (NCLB) has been replaced with the Every Student Succeeds Act (ESSA), which reauthorizes NCLB and adds, among other items, "College and Career Ready Standards," "Innovative Local Assessment Pilot," and "Teacher and Leader Evaluation Systems." The Illinois Genocide Education Mandate has been all but forgotten at Lincoln. Content standards have been pushed aside to make space for the new accountability measures. Illinois among other states are at the beginning of the new Common Core State Standards initiative by the National Governors Association, which means a new set of standards and a new test, the Partnership for Assessment and State Readiness for College and Careers (PARCC). PARCC is defined on its website as follows: "a group of states working together to develop a set of assessments that measure whether students are on track to be successful in college and their careers." It is a computer-based K–12 assessment. This year, our school will spend three weeks rotating nearly one thousand students through reading and math testing rooms. Students will spend almost ten hours testing and, in my case, won't have reading class for a week. For the last two years, Lincoln's school district has spent countless hours and resources training teachers to implement the new standards, including spending professional development time taking the PARCC tests ourselves.

During the 2012–2013 school year, at a time when our school was abandoning Illinois State Standards and not quite responsible for Common Core, and at a time when we had just changed administrators for the fifth time in nine years, I proposed to our incoming principal that I wanted to reimagine the English classroom. I wanted to make our year about using reading and writing to examine the social forces that are shaping our understanding of society and our place in the world. I wanted to avoid materials that work to constrain learning: worksheets, packets, and multiple-choice and fill-in-the-blank tests. I wanted to hide the textbooks and abridged texts and use primary sources. And I did not want to do any test prep or make our work about grades or points. For a number of reasons—our failing school report card, a concern for student engagement in the textbook, a competing force of gang life, and an increase in student hospitalizations—the principal supported the idea.

As part of my plan, I was not going to teach a unit on the Holocaust or genocide explicitly; I planned to make our year about uncovering how literature represents humanity. I wanted to let literature do the work. I wanted students to see reading as more than vocabulary and writing as more than grammar. The mandate to teach a unit of instruction on genocide is not about saying "we covered genocide" any more than the standards have to be about saying "I covered text evidence." Teaching English is about teaching how language constructs and imposes certain ways of knowing. Rhetoric and witnessing became the foundations for work, but I had to figure out how to use the principle of rhetoric and witnessing, seemingly more applicable to nonfiction, in the reading of fiction. How can we read fiction rhetorically? What is the responsibility of the reader to a story of fiction? And when writing about genocide, what is the author's responsibility to the subject and her reader in representing human rights violations?

What Does a Novel Do?

Martha Nussbaum, philosopher and professor of law and ethics, argues that the novel engages us in the contemplation of lives different from our own and expands our imaginative capabilities so that we may better make judgments about what society *ought* to be. A literary imagination is "an essential ingredient" for human beings to concern themselves with the *good* of other people. Reading novels, she argues, can help people imagine society in ways they otherwise wouldn't by representing people and places excluded from public consciousnesses. Reading genocide literature in middle and secondary classrooms can help people better understand the nature of language and its causes, but it can also nurture in readers a capacity to respond to its meaning (or intended effect) more effectively and humanely. Thus, in this chapter I explore how reading novels, specifically genocide novels, can develop in our students a conscious imagination for future social action. I make an argument for reading novels in the English classroom to develop a conscious imagination in our students rather than to focus on reading skills. This is not to say I ignored the standards; no, I took this opportunity between reform eras to explore how standards can be used in the service of understanding literature and how it represents humanity.

A genocide novel imaginatively represents subjects, people, and history using narrative techniques (e.g., dialogue, sensory language, typography) and imaginative methods less common to nonfiction (e.g., fictionality, nonreferential individuals, third-person narrator, split subjectivity). The aesthetic of a genocide novel demands different epistemological and ethical responsibilities of the reader than nonfiction because of its fictionality, as I will discuss below. The author is not a survivor of genocide, and so the reader is not aligned as the listener of historical testimony. The aesthetic of fiction distances the reader from a real witness in order to ask the reader to imagine that which is beyond or in the gaps of the imagined survivor's testimony.

Readers of genocide novels enter a narrative plane to practice and nurture social action because they imagine and explore the cultural, political, social, economic, and environmental factors that come into play before, during, and after genocidal processes. Winfried Fluck, a professor of American studies in Berlin, writes, "The fictional text is a medium for expressing a sense of injustice while making up for the experiences of injustice by increased recognition and by establishing justice on a symbolic level" (22). For Nussbaum and Fluck, then, the novel can be a mechanism for justice because the novel is especially good at helping us recognize injustices, imagine more just alternatives, and work toward those alternatives.

To be clear, the conscious imagination is an essential element of the reading process but of also social action. Our imagination, and all our life experiences that color our imagination, interacts with the symbols on the page to create images in our minds, images that become part of our memory. Teaching fiction with a sense of rhetoricality means we teach our students to be conscious of the way their imaginations are being influenced, how we can better understand the ways our imaginations transact with the aesthetic of the text (video game, film, television program), and how we can uncover the ethics of such reading encounters. If we are to be conscious of how our imagination is engaged by fiction to envision and contemplate society, we must, as English teachers, develop ways to illuminate the aesthetic, ethics, and rhetorical qualities of the reading experience.

Imagining Justice in the Classroom

One of the benefits of novels is that they grant us imaginative access to experiences we would not otherwise have. In *Poetic Justice*, Nussbaum goes so far as to suggest our politicians and legislators (whom she calls "Guardians") *ought* to read imaginative literature to develop the necessary sympathy to recognize "the irreducible singularity of each human being and the qualitative aspects of each person's experience" (32). Narratives produce a sort of enlightenment as they draw us into sympathetic involvement with the characters as individuals, eliciting our sympathy to inspire and lead readers into the public for *right* action.

Reading a novel, the literary experience, is akin to "reading the world" as Paolo Freire wrote. We must, at one time, relate to the humanity of others across time and space while recognizing their mode of expression as "social fictions," for language is never quite adequate to the expression of its meaning (Richards). Unlike nonfiction literature, a novel cannot rely on the "been there" quality of a testimony that obliges the reader to attend to the witness, nor does a novel pretend to have "been there." The beautiful problem of fiction is that while it engages us in the contemplation of lives different from our own and while it expands our imaginative capabilities, it acknowledges its fiction. The reader is not aligned to the writer as with testimonial literature; instead, the reader experiences, on different levels and at different times, detachment or a distance that enables her to get a more refined sense of what her emotions actually are and to sort out beliefs and intuitions better (Nussbaum 69). While the art object is fiction, the literary experience of reading a novel and the contemplation it evokes are real. Thus, for Nussbaum (and for me), the imaginative literary experiences afforded by novels promote habits of mind that, if read with attention to reading response, rhetoricality, and witnessing, might dismantle institutions and beliefs that perpetuate inequality, injustice, and violence (92).

Considering Louise Rosenblatt's theoretical perspective on transactional reading theory, I think Rosenblatt would agree with Nussbaum in that novels encourage readers to contemplate their values as human beings and members of society. In *Literature as Exploration*, Rosenblatt says, "The implied moral attitudes and unvoiced systems of social values are reinforced by the persuasiveness of art" (8). Texts embody these "implied" ethical and cultural attitudes and values, and so teachers have the responsibility to teach students how to negotiate the "persuasiveness" or rhetorical terrain of the art object. Students need space to respond to texts, to notice how their lives and experiences transact with the plane, to feel the emotional, ethical, and logical appeals of the text. (See Chapter 10 for a classroom example.) For Rosenblatt, "Teaching becomes a matter of improving the individual's capacity to evoke meaning from the text by leading him to reflect self-critically on this process" (26). "This process" includes how a fictional narrative moves us and teaches us in ways that are far from fictional. The conscious imagination recognizes that images and texts invite us to imagine people and places outside our lives and experiences and that while those images and texts make people, places, and ideas accessible to us, they are created by human beings who have intentions with ethical implications.

As with testimonial literature, genocide fiction can perpetuate stereotypes of distant others and dehumanize victims and survivors by spectacularizing the human rights violations. The sympathy-eliciting function of narratives can lead readers into the "wrong" direction or can be misappropriated for unethical purposes. If we consider Hesford's *Spectacular Rhetorics*, we will remember that narratives can enact a spectacle of human rights violations, exploiting the victim to provoke sympathy. Indeed, how productive is sympathy that projects and perpetuates exclusion? Thus, while I suggest that the novel expands our imaginative capabilities (e.g., imagining how society *ought* to be), the novel can also perpetuate narrow views of society (e.g., stereotypes). The modern English classroom, then, must take up the task of uncovering the way imaginative texts represent justice and injustice. Readers might ask: Is the author's representation exploiting the victim? What is the author's purpose in depicting a particularly graphic scene in the novel? Our project, and our ethical responsibility as teachers, is to make conscious the imagination of genocide novels.

In making textual representations conscious, the English classroom can ensure these exercises of the imagination (which come through reading novels) direct our imaginations in productive ways. The way we can best assure the proper exercise of imagination is to pay attention to the ethical, aesthetic, and rhetorical appeals (emotional, ethical, and rational) of fiction. In a novel, the epistemological and ethical concerns are in the fictional representation of genocide. While the state may want students to be "college and career ready," I suggest that we, as a society, should want more or, at minimum, shape how we define "ready." We want students to go into those colleges and careers with an understanding of the social forces that shape our existence and the lives of people across the globe—lives that are increasingly interdependent. We want students to develop an imagination for how our world *ought* to be.

The Rhetorical Aesthetic of Fiction

If English teachers will accept the argument that the English classroom is a site to nurture in our students a conscious imagination, which allows us to imagine just relationships and circumstances, then our use of the imagination in reading novels to promote justice necessarily involves attention to the aesthetics of fiction. In this section, I look at the aesthetic of fiction in the novel beginning with the early eighteenth century and consider the way this genre negotiates fact and deception and can cultivate in readers a conscious imagination.

Misson and Morgan see aesthetic as transactional; it "entails a creator, the work created, and an audience" (33). In other words, for Misson and Morgan, aesthetic is not located in the stimuli (the art object) or in the responder but in the transactional space where they intersect and produce perception. The aesthetic of fiction refers to the interactions among the creator, the work created, and the audience that produce perception. The aesthetic of fiction is not static; it is never stable. Aesthetic is dynamic, open to insight and discovery with each reader and reading event.

I will begin with "the work created" in order to define two terms that are central to a rhetorical reading of novels: "fiction" and "novel." Fiction, according to the Oxford Dictionaries, is defined as an "invention or fabrication as opposed to fact"; in addition, fiction is "literature in the form of prose, especially short stories and novels that describes imaginary events and people." A "novel" is "a fictitious prose narrative of book length, typically representing character and action with some degree of realism." According to Catharine Gallagher in "The Rise of Fictionality," the second use of "fiction" and this definition of "novel" came into existence around the turn of the seventeenth century. By the mid-eighteenth century, "an explicit and ongoing discourse of fictionality" developed in British narratives (337). Gallagher suggests that the nature of fictionality changed in these narratives to constitute a new form that readers today still anticipate when picking up a novel. Initially, fiction was associated with genres such as fables and fairy tales that made no claims to realism and would not be accused of deception; prior to the eighteenth century, few readers had trouble recognizing fiction for this reason. Gallagher explains, "When the obvious nonexistence of its reference separated it from both truth and falsehood, even the most naïve readers could recognize fiction" (338). In other words, fiction was unproblematic for readers because of its "blatant incredibility." By the early eighteenth century, as some authors experimented with more realistic forms of fiction, any narrative that did not contain talking animals or flying carpets but did seem referential was accused of fraud. Readers new to the transactions across fiction and realism had trouble deciphering fact and fiction, and some novelists were accused of libel and deception. The ethics of realist fiction troubled both readers and writers because a "conceptual category of fiction" was lacking and because the stories did not "solicit belief" (340). The work created, the novel, needed the reader and the writer to imagine how to negotiate the real and the fiction.

The "creator" or the novelist avoided being a libeler by renouncing references to real individuals. Instead, novelists imagined and created fictional individuals, understanding that the novel's realism depended on the "over fictitiousness of its particulars" (342). Gallagher explains:

> The fictionality defining the novel inhered in the *creation* of instances, rather than their mere selection, to illustrate a class of person. Because a general referent was indicated through a particular, but explicitly nonreferential, fictional individual, the novel could be judged generally true even though all of its particulars are merely imaginary.
>
> (342)

Thus, with a new category of fiction and some parameters to avoid fraud, the novelists of the time moved toward more credible settings and believable stories. The novel's aesthetic of plausibility above reality became a mechanism for novelists to negotiate fact and deception.

Once novelists had a category of fiction (one with plausibility) that allowed them to represent reality, British authors of the time used the novel to represent the human condition, a human condition that represented the lives of people reading novels and the lives of people who could not. Some authors critiqued modernity, social and economic progress, by exposing the sickness and poverty of modernity's darker side (De Foe's *The Fortunes and Misfortunes of the Famous Moll Flanders*). Such novels created in readers a capacity to sympathize with the distress of the other and to contemplate aspects of society perhaps not previously perceived by the classes able to read and afford novels. By calling attention to its fiction, authors nurtured in readers a capacity to perceive a human condition caused and perpetuated by modern mechanisms through characters marginalized by modernity (who were not able to read novels). What is interesting to note, however, is that the mode for critiquing modernity (i.e., fiction) featured traits encouraged by modernity: "disbelief, speculation, and credit" (346). Thus, in doing so, as Gallagher points out, the early novel emphasized "gullibility, innocence deceived, rash promises extracted, and impetuous and financial investments" (346). The aesthetic of fiction once defined by "blatant incredibility" began to "solicit belief." In a way, the novel began to unveil the rhetoric of the time for people to first imagine in the privacy of their reading experience and then, perhaps, to witness in public spaces.

As the novel and the novelist changed, the reader's ability to decipher fact from fiction progressed, and her responsibility to the novel's fictionality took on a critical dimension. At first, novel readers sympathized with innocent credulity; however, the practice of reading, of negotiating the real and the fiction, developed a conscious disbelief. The reader developed a capacity for anticipating problems, making suppositional predictions, seeing possible outcomes and alternate interpretations. The eighteenth-century reader was positioned to speculate on the action and hypothesize about it. In sum, fictionality began to nurture (and continues to nurture today) a conscious disbelief, which prompts judgments "not about the story's reality, but about its *believability*, its plausibility" (Gallagher 347).

The aesthetic of fiction urges a reader to suspend disbelief while inviting the reader to speculate on the action. In reading a novel in the English classroom, we call attention to the work as fiction so that its aesthetic is about believability or plausibility rather than reality. What is "reality" or "real" when it comes to representing our world through language? Can language ever wholly capture an experience or "what happened"? At the beginning of the nineteenth century, Coleridge said, "fiction solicits a *willing* suspension of disbelief, and this sensation of individual control over disbelief set novel-reading apart from other acts of skepticism" (Gallagher 347). For Coleridge, the will of a human being is the key. While Gallagher points out that the novel has been accused of "seducing its readers into imaginary experiences that were remarkably hard to exit" (348), Coleridge seemed to have more faith in the novel reader. For Coleridge, belief is a judgment that cannot be made without will; engrossed as we may be in a novel, we are conscious of its fiction. In my view, the beauty of fiction is what Gallagher names a paradox:

> The novel gives us explicit fiction and simultaneously seems to occlude it; the novel reader opens what she knows is a fiction because it is a

> fiction and soon finds that enabling knowledge to be the subtlest of the experiences' elements. Just as it declares itself, it becomes that which goes without saying.
>
> (349)

In sum, since the beginning of the novel, there have been ethical considerations with representing the real in a form defined by its imaginary such as fraud and deception. The creator, the work created, and the reader are part of the aesthetic of fiction and are thus compelled to negotiate questions of deception and plausibility. In my experience teaching with and learning from genocide literature this past decade, the ethical concerns of genocide novels create a framework for responding to genocide. Lawrence Langer, in *The Holocaust and the Literary Imagination*, writes,

> the art of atrocity is a stubbornly unsettling art, indifferent to the peace that passeth understanding and intent only on reclaiming for the present, not the experience of the horror itself . . . but a framework for responding to it, for making it *imaginatively* (if not literally) accessible.
>
> (Langer's emphasis, 12)

The art is the work of the artist, who, in the case of fiction (as opposed to memoir or autobiography) having not "been there," can focus on them (the events) rationally and imaginatively (20). The aim of the genocide novel is not to shock the reader so that she cannot react to the work or to the atrocity; the purpose should be to facilitate the beginnings of a response, to carve out in our minds a memory of the atrocity so that it is not forgotten. If we think back to Chapter 3 (rhetoricality), we recall that people use language to serve different political and ideological interests and opposing causes. Thus, when reading genocide novels, readers are negotiating deception and plausibility so that they are not implicated in a cause that perpetuates injustice or in a shallow understanding of the complexity of our human condition (e.g., stereotypes, victimization, nationalism).

The Ethics of Imagining Genocide

As English teachers in middle and high schools, should we read with our students texts that imagine the conditions of genocide? Might a fictional account of genocide offend a survivor? Why read fiction when we have testimonial literature?

The English classroom is the ideal site to illuminate the tension between aesthetics and ethics in the production of art that represents genocide. This tension is best articulated by the highly cited phrase by Holocaust survivor Theodor Adorno who, in 1949, said, "to write poetry after Auschwitz is barbaric" (162). Adorno asks how an artist-author presumes to represent something as extreme as genocide when one cannot do so without, in some way, depicting the values of the systems that produced it and the biases still present in societies around the world. Adorno's concern gets at the heart of ethical reading and the problem of standards and accountability. To consider how authors represent our world is an endeavor for which English teachers and students are well suited. And in asking ethical questions of representation, we also consider what it would mean to not "write poetry." After all, isn't it a necessity to write so that we do not forget? But what are we remembering? How are we remembering it? And what are we to do with an imagination conscious of the darkest deeds of humankind? What a worthwhile project for the English classroom.

With the subject of genocide, the artist-author has a responsibility to her subject and her readers to ethically negotiate the forces of historical fact and imaginative truth in her medium. The task of the artist, then, is to make that which is never wholly invented or factual a reality possible for the imagination. On one hand, the "fiction" might be perceived by survivors in the way Imre Kertesz suggests, "the survivors watch helplessly as their only real possessions are done away with: authentic experiences" (269). Indeed, a novel representing genocide may offend the survivors of genocide. On the other hand, survivor accounts have their limit, and an artist-author may create a plausible account of what happened to those who did not survive and of atrocities not otherwise accessible to our minds. As Primo Levi wrote in *If This Is a Man*, an account of the year he spent as a prisoner in Auschwitz:

> We, survivors, are not the true witnesses . . . [W]e are those who by their prevarications or abilities or good luck did not touch bottom. Those who did so, those who saw the Gorgon, have not returned to tell about it. (63–64)

As survivors, then, they did not, in the case of the Holocaust, go to the gas chamber or know what was happening in other camps or countries. Through fiction and the aesthetic experience of reading, the true horrors of genocide (i.e., without surviving witnesses) can be depicted and understood as an aesthetic experience to become part of the memory of generations living in its aftermath. The questions of how an author negotiated historical fact and imaginative truth and whether the object created is a just representation of the Gorgon is, in my view, a valuable and ethical line of inquiry for the English classroom because it nurtures a capacity for questioning the way human rights violations are represented in all mediums and the cause such representations serve. How is the artist imagining the subject and representing it in this medium, the novel? How does this art object ask us to imagine lives, time, and places different from our own? What theory about society does this art object invite us to contemplate?

The ethics of imagining genocide, specifically, and the ethics of imagining more broadly are a concern for readers so that they are not drawn into the spectacle of violence or distant suffering (Hesford). For Berel Lang in

Holocaust Representations: Art within the Limits of History and Ethics, that means "how to justify what *is* spoken" (my emphasis 19), and for Thomas Trezise in "Unspeakable," that means "not *whether* but *how* it should be represented" (my emphasis 43). In 1975, Lawrence L. Langer, in *The Holocaust and the Literary Imagination*, makes a unique contribution to literary criticism by introducing "literature of atrocity," which includes literature written by survivors and nonsurvivors, fiction and nonfiction. I have named this genre genocide literature to call attention to the rhetoricality of the word "genocide," but Langer and I both mean to call attention to how this body of literature has devised an idiom and style for the unspeakable.

Langer's work attempts to impose some critical order on selected imaginative works around the themes of the aesthetic problem of reconciling normalcy with horror, the displacement of the consciousness of life by the immanence and pervasiveness of death, the violation of childhood, the assault on physical reality, the distinction of rational intelligence, and the disruption of chronological time. In considering these "problems," he is noting the ethical nature of representation and the authority of the artist-author over these problems. Langer explains the aesthetic and ethical endeavor of such "Art":

> [I]t is not its transfiguration of empirical reality but its disfiguration, the conscious and deliberate alienation of the reader's sensibilities from the world of the usual and familiar, with an accompanying infiltration into the work of the grotesque, the senseless, and the unimaginable, to such a degree that the possibility of aesthetic pleasure . . . is intrinsically eliminated. (3)

The principle of aesthetic stylization such as the sequence and structure of an experience is one way that art forces us to search for more adequate bases for apprehending the human suffering. Langer seems to be suggesting that some artists, in representing atrocity, create aesthetic distance by "infiltration" of the "grotesque" and "unimaginable" in order to prevent or minimize a pleasurable response from readers. However, it seems to me that such an approach is risky in that the horror will shock the reader or cause her to turn away, leaving her numb and incapable of a response that might foster conscious deliberation. On the other hand, to push for the *unfamiliar*, to not attempt to recreate the horror, might be a way of covering up the inadequacy of our imaginations when confronted with genocide. Thus, some artists, as nonwitnesses who do not and cannot know the horror of genocide, rely on the *usual* and *familiar* to show that genocide can and does repeat itself in a society structured like ours. Zygmunt Bauman, who argues the Holocaust was rooted in modernity, writes,

> The truth is that every "ingredient" of the Holocaust—all those things that rendered it possible—was normal . . . in the sense of being fully in

> keeping with everything we know about our civilization, its guiding spirit, its priorities, its immanent vision of the world.
>
> (9)

Seen this way, the Holocaust and genocide, are not moments of "barbarism" in our history but a development of modern culture that continues today, and so in representing genocide, artists can refrain from attempting (and failing) to represent the unimaginable by portraying the familiar.

When reading genocide literature, teachers and students will see examples of artists attempting "deliberate alienation" with the grotesque and authors relying on the familiar to show the genocidal processes of everyday life, but for Elie Wiesel in *Against Silence*, it is not one or the other: "The aim of every book, of every tale is to initiate as many encounters on as many levels as possible: between the writer and reader, speaker and listener, fact and fiction, imagination and reality, past and present" (1:310). Readers with a conscious imagination can judge which aesthetic stylization is more ethical. In reading a variety of genocide literature, teachers and students can uncover the varied ways artists make sense of "our civilization."

The fictionality in a novel has the advantage of making it possible to convey what happens at the moment of death or defy spatial constraints by conveying parallel experiences. The choices are the artist-author's art. The novel is a form of representation that reminds us that the imaginary is constructed, and it asks of readers and their imaginations to consider the ethics of that construction. In effect, fictional representations of genocide provide a framework for contemplating in the English classroom the ethics of the imaginary. And finally, the aesthetic of fiction in novel form offers a framework for ethical *reasoning*. Teaching and reading are ethical endeavors. The claim of fiction is that the literary imagination is an essential part of both the theory and practice of humanity balancing emotional response and rational thought. Nussbaum cites Wayne Booth in explaining the act of reading as "ethically valuable" because, she says, "it is constructed in a manner that demands both immersion and critical conversation" (9). Specifically, Nussbaum sees the novel as a genre that constructs a paradigm of ethical reasoning that is context specific without being relativistic, in which we bring the general idea of humanity to bear on a concrete situation, which we are invited to enter through imagination. If we think of reading in this way, as combining one's own absorbed imagining with periods of more detached critical scrutiny, we can begin to see how the aesthetic of fiction prepares us to contemplate ethical representations of genocide specifically and the human condition more broadly (Nussbaum 9).

Conclusion

While I do think a novel is a form of art to be appreciated for its aesthetic value, I also think that this art has pedagogical potential to not only teach about something but enact the problematic of trying to teach about something. In other words, the novel cultivates in readers a consciousness of language as a representation of what is real rather than some absolute truth or fact. The novel is a narrative that accounts for voices and experiences while inevitably leaving gaps for the reader—spaces that cannot actually be known or accounted for but invite deliberation and wonder. I would like to emphasize that certain teaching practices—that is, ones that recognize and underscore that our knowledge is always partial, ones that embrace ambiguity and explore questions rather than try to find definite answers—are consistent with the way in which the novel embodies the fluidity of language.

Reading genocide literature in middle and secondary classrooms, therefore, can work to make visible the meaning-making process not only of texts but of our world. To grasp that language is never real but a representation of the real requires a conscious imagination. The practice of reading novels promotes habits of mind that have the potential to dismantle oppressive institutions and beliefs that perpetuate injustice and violence in the world. The fictionality of novels offers the English classroom a framework for ethical reasoning that can be expanded to other subjects and mediums.

What follows are three rhetorical readings of the aesthetic of fiction in genocide novels. You will notice that while I have separated the examples by rhetorical appeals (ethical, emotional, and rational), all three appeals are present in each text. And while I analyze authorial choices, I am also analyzing the work created and considering its impact on the implied reader—again, to demonstrate the dynamic nature of aesthetic and the reading process. In each instance, I consider the ethical questions author-artists consider when representing genocide, the ethical implications of their choices, and the responsibility of the reader to recognize how the artist-author is attending to the details of the past, treating the experiences of survivors, and caring for the consciousness of her young readers.

Works Cited

Adorno, Theodor. *Can One Live After Auschwitz? A Philosophical Reader.* Ed. Rolf Tiedeman. Trans. Rodney Livingstone. Stanford: Stanford University Press, 2003. Print.

Bauman, Zygmunt. *Modernity and the Holocaust.* Ithaca, NY: Cornell University Press, 1989. Print.

Booth, Wayne C. *The Rhetoric of Fiction.* Chicago: University of Chicago, 1961. Print.

Every Student Succeeds Act (ESSA). 2015. Web.

Fluck, Winfried. "Fiction and Justice." *New Literary History.* 34.1 (2003): 19–42. Print.

Freire, Paulo. *Pedagogy of the Oppressed.* New York: Seabury Press, 1970. Print.

Gallagher, Catherine. "The Rise of Fictionality." Ed. Franco Moretti. *The Novel: History, Geography, and Culture.* Princeton: Princeton University Press, 2006. 336–363. Print.

Hesford, Wendy S. *Spectacular Rhetorics: Human Rights Visions, Recognitions, Feminisms.* Durham, NC: Duke University Press, 2011. Print.

Kertesz, I., and MacKay, J. "Who Owns Auschwitz?" *The Yale Journal of Criticism.* 14.1 (2001): 267–272. 15 May 2016. Web.

Lang, Berel. *Holocaust Representation: Art Within the Limits of History and Ethics.* Baltimore, MD: The John Hopkins Press, 2000. Print.
Langer, Lawrence. *The Holocaust and the Literary Imagination.* New Haven, CT: Yale University Press, 1975. Print.
Levi, Primo. *If This Is a Man and the Truce.* London: Little, Brown Book Group, 1991. Print.
Misson, Ray, and Wendy Morgan. *Critical Literacy and the Aesthetic: Transforming the English Classroom.* Urbana, IL: NCTE, 2006. Print.
National Governors Association. "Common Core State Standards Initiative." *Corestandards.org.* 27 Oct. 2012. Web.
Nussbaum, Martha C. *Poetic Justice: The Literary Imagination and Public Life.* Boston: Beacon Press, 1995. Print.
Oxford Dictionaries. Oxford: Oxford University Press, 2016. Web.
Partnership for Assessment of Readiness for College and Careers. PARCC, Inc. 2015. Web.
Richards, I. A. *Poetries and Sciences.* London: Routledge, 1970. Print.
Rosenblatt, Louise. *Literature as Exploration.* New York: Appleton Century, 1938. 4th ed. New York: Modern Language Association, 1983. Print.
Trezise, Thomas. "Unspeakable." *Yale Journal of Criticism.* 14 (2001): 38–63. Print.
Wiesel, Elie. *Against Silence: The Voice and Vision of Elie Wiesel, Volume 1.* Ann Arbor, MI: Holocaust Library, 1985. Web.

6 The Ethics of a Child Narrator

English teachers unfamiliar with genocide may wonder how to go about selecting "good" genocide novels. Ruth Gilbert, in "Grasping the Unimaginable" (2010), argues that overtly didactic novels can close down a "child reader's imaginative engagement with the ungraspable nature" of the Holocaust, specifically (355). Her recommendation is to select novels for the classroom that confront the reader with a "complex set of ideas about the relationship between narrative and subjectivity" (357); she argues experiencing this confrontation as a reader is actually more educative than novels that attempt to "impose order on chaos by presenting neat seamless narrative structures" (357). According to Gilbert, then, teachers should select novels that offer a representation of ambiguity and uncertainty in life. This approach to selecting curriculum respects not only the complexity of genocide but the nature of adolescence, which is wrought with the discomfort of uncertainty.

If literary writing can draw young readers into this representation rather than being a conduit of information, the novel will actually be doing something quite remarkable; it will "capture the fractured nature" of not only global atrocities like genocide but modern life (Gilbert 355). However, it is important for students to read texts that represent genocide in a variety of ways. Reading "neat" representations of humanity with students offers an opportunity to call attention to the rhetoricality of texts and contemplate the ethics of representation, including the aesthetic value of the novel as an art object. Whether the author is attempting a complex representation of humanity or a simple representation, the scene of address is manipulated for the audience and is, thus, an opportunity for the audience to become conscious of the actions that create such a scene.

The ability of literature to create characters is a unique and powerful rhetorical tool. It can enable an author who did not witness firsthand genocide to speak through a created personality with a stronger ethical appeal. According to Mannix,

> [Literature] can place the personality of the character, and, therefore, his ethical appeal, at the very heart of the artistic experience. If that

> personality changes as the result of the conflicts that the novel presents him with and if these changes somehow enlighten us, we have an artistic work with a high thematic content. If we feel compelled to change an opinion or take some action on the basis of our experience of the character's transformation, we have a literary and rhetorical artifact.
>
> (46)

The artist-author determines the rhetorical modality of the narrator's speech and what kind of witness he will be as the narrator. Genette explains this as focalization—the degree to which the narrator is aware and the extent to which her knowledge is restricted. This modality of knowledge is about the narrator's position or outside-ness in relation to the story. To what degree can a character witness the genocide process, and to what degree must the narrator, relying on research or real witness accounts, tell about these events? Such is the narrative modality of knowledge. Narration relates the story, but it does not accept the mark of truth, which is to say that the story does not become necessarily relative but that it recognizes the limits of the subject's knowledge and experiences.

When teaching teenagers—who are grappling with identity and their place in the world and are impressionable and sensitive and at different stages of maturation—the ethical appeal seems *that* much more important. Is it exploiting the death of genocide victims for the sake of reader engagement? The attention that artists pay to their selection of characters and characterization is a tribute to the continuing importance of the ethical appeal in fiction, specifically fiction that explores the darker side of modernity such as genocide literature.

Written by Patricia McCormick, *Never Fall Down* (2012) is a novel, or *fictional* account, about Arn Chorn-Pond's experiences as a child soldier in the killing fields of Cambodia. Here, I would like to consider how McCormick negotiates fictionalizing a historical account of the Cambodian genocide (1975–1979) and the rhetorical effect. Of concern to middle and high school English teachers is how authors writing for a young-adult audience provide a literary and educative experience while not overwhelming them. If the author is not a witness of genocide, the ethical appeal must come through the characters and landscape created by the author. When writing a novel about genocide, the author is likely attempting to move the reader to change an opinion or take some social action. At minimum, the change might simply be a kinder disposition toward our fellow human beings, but ideally, a young reader might go on to be an activist. The content, however, is incredibly sensitive, and not all students are ready to face human rights atrocities either because of maturity levels or because they, too, experienced trauma in their lives. In writing young-adult novels about genocide, then, what authorial strategies does Patricia McCormick use to create ethical appeal, and what are the ethical implications of her authorial choices?

One strategy for writing about genocide for young audiences is to write a fictionalized account from a child's point of view. According to Sarah Jordan in "Educating Without Overwhelming: Authorial Strategies in Children's Holocaust Literature" (2005), the young reader will be able to take on "for a moment, the perspective of a child who lived during the Holocaust and perhaps begin to address their own question of what it was like and how it could have happened" (200). While narrating the story from a child's point of view is powerful, it offers a subject for critical review. At one point, Jordan cites Totten, a leading genocide education scholar, as saying that literature can help personalize history as a way of facing inhumanity in a human way; however, she neglects to note that Totten also says that it is insufficient to seek empathy for that which is impossible to imagine let alone experience vicariously. Perhaps for this reason Jordan suggests that effective literature about genocide should do much more than edit the graphic details or tell about what happened. The novel defies such economy.

If an objective of young-adult literature is for today's children to identify with children of the past, child-narrated stories that show the similarities in growing up (e.g., interest in ice cream, love of games, being sweet on the cute girl in class, sibling rivalry) personalize history and make the events more believable. Fiction is less about believability and more about plausibility. Because child narrators often do not know much about what is happening or why beyond what they see and experience, the reader can at once find the child's observations plausible while recognizing the child's understanding of the history or events as provisional. For example, in *Never Fall Down*, Arn, the narrator/protagonist, talks to us about how he sells ice cream for extra money and how he spies on his rich neighbor: "But one girl in the window, the same age as me, the one with eyeglass, sometime she stick her tongue at me. And now I think maybe I love her a little bit" (16). Young readers identify with Arn, and perhaps they are enlightened by how a distant other experiences childhood, how the innocence of childhood defies geography.

Children are also quite perceptive; they have agency even though some human rights narratives depict children as wholly naïve. Arn has some sense of the political unrest in Cambodia at the beginning of the novel: "Truck full of soldier ride down the street shouting in a bullhorn. 'We are Khmer Rouge,' they say. 'We are Red Cambodia.' Also they say the prince is coming back, that all government soldier [sic] should come meet him at the airport" (12). Young readers are confused and left wondering what this all means, as is Arn; McCormick elicits this tension in her readers through her narrator. Both the characters and the readers are in the dark, so there is some equal footing and a sympathetic alignment. Like most of the people in Cambodia at the time, Arn has no idea what the Khmer Rouge is planning, but as the plan unfolds, Arn learns the rules for survival, and his readers learn, too—alongside him. Arn begins to piece together what he has heard and what he sees as his readers do. There is no adult or omniscient narrator to help Arn tell the "truth" of what is happening; he is experiencing and telling at the same time. In other words, there is no narratorial or experiential distance in this novel with this child-narrator.

The lack of narratorial distance, in my view, poses an ethical problem for some educators who might be considering *Never Fall Down* as a novel to read with all their students (i.e., whole class). While the protagonist has strong ethical appeal, and while it is realistic *fiction*, the present-tense narration of the most unimaginable circumstances might overwhelm young readers, a key criticism in young-adult genocide novels. The argument for violence in young adult novels more generally is to mirror teens' lives or give a voice to traumatized teens or voiceless victims. Reading about other teens can be validating or comforting. On the other hand, there is a danger in normalizing certain behaviors and experiences, making what Gallagher calls "plausibility" appear as reality. I do not think these arguments necessarily apply to young-adult genocide novels because fiction, as a medium, explicitly invites deliberation between fact and deception. I think that the fictional narrator, Arn, invites his reader to *imagine* she is his secondhand witness to the child soldier experience; the reader is not asked to experience it or to completely grasp it.

Because the narrator is so matter-of-fact, even detached at times, the reader is always uncomfortable and thus aware of the imaginative nature of the text. For example, Arn, the narrator, does not edit what he sees for his listener, nor does he make any apologies as if unaware of the age or culture of his imagined listeners. We know that adolescents mature at different times and different ways, and so while some novels hint at the truth behind details, Arn tells his listener exactly what he witnesses, thus allowing his listener to also bear witness from a distance:

> In the square I see this new guy, white shorts, no shirt, and six soldier. Also ten guys down on knees, hands tied, all naked, in a row. The guy in the white shorts, he has a gun with a knife attach, a bayonet. He point the bayonet at the chest of one guy in the row. Then very quick, he slice the skin and pull out the liver. So quick, so neat, the liver, it stick on the end of the knife. The kneeling guy, he's still living; his liver not inside him anymore—in front of his face. Crying, only saying, "No, no, no," Then he fall down.
>
> (76)

McCormick is not allowing Arn to be ignorant here nor veiling the event as some authors of Holocaust literature do to make it age appropriate (as Jordan notes). The narrator, Arn, is not unaware, nor is there an adult to filter or interpret the details; he presents the event as an eyewitness to the atrocities without interpretation. This seems like an authorial risk for McCormick. Jordan's selections for age-appropriate Holocaust literature celebrate texts that do not quite engage with the "harsh reality outside the imagined adventure" (204), keeping the child hidden physically and emotionally from the events to teach about life, death, and survival by resisting graphic images. I think those strategies weaken the character's ethical appeal and insult the reader. Arn's narratorial voice, one that is somewhat detached emotionally, is McCormick's strategy for representing survival, how Arn managed to "never fall down" by recounting what was visible yet still incomprehensible.

In Chapter 6 of *Never Fall Down*, readers go deeper into the landscape of the Khmer Rouge's "Year Zero," four years into methodical murder, and four years of Arn trying to "never fall down." Arn reports this scene about a "wandering boy" who leaves the hut at night:

> I look for him everywhere. By the side of the hut, in the kitchen. I see a light, a small light, in the mango grove. A bad smell there, and sometimes the bodies get bloat and blow up and pop out of the ground. I'm scared of that place, scared of ghost, but I go anyway. And I see the wandering boy. I see him crouching, holding arm of a dead guy, chewing. I don't know how long he been doing that, eating the flesh, the human flesh; but now I know why he always asleep in the morning.
>
> (87)

While this scene is of the graphic nature that Jordan considers overwhelming for young readers, it is essential in moving the protagonist to a realization. It places the personality of the character and his ethical appeal at the heart of the literary experience. Up until this point in the novel, Arn has slowly become "famous" in the camp for his ability to sing, play the *khim*, and lead a group of musicians in Angkar songs. He has gained some power in the camp to be allowed out at night because of his "fame," a power of voice to speak up and even save his fellow musicians, who would otherwise be killed because of their poor musical skills. But even though he sees this wandering boy near the mangrove trees, Arn cannot use his "power" to save; the image unveiled some truth of humanity for Arn, a hopelessness, maybe a reality that he had compartmentalized in order to survive. He says, after witnessing the above scene: "Now I am a ghost" (87).

What is this novel doing, then, that an informational text cannot? Arn Chorn-Pond has written autobiographical accounts of his experiences as a child soldier in the killing fields, yet he permitted McCormick to mediate his story and render it as a novel. The aesthetic of fiction is its plausibility, which holds at bay notions of reality and creates what Gallagher calls "cognitive provisionality." We cannot imagine the suffering of the distant other, and yet we must if we are to recognize that genocide is not an accident of history but mass murder made possible because of choices individuals, organizations, and governments made. There is nothing "realistic" about the following images, and yet readers know (cognitively) they are being confronted with the darkness of humanity:

> New prisoner coming to the camp all the time. No hiding them anymore. Now the Khmer Rouge take them right through the square. Tie together, head low. They beat them in front of us so we can see what happens to people with bad character. Always the Khmer Rouge watch us, all the time. They watch to see if you show any emotion to the victim. You do, they will kill you.
>
> (90)

> "These people, they no good," says one Khmer Rouge. "They old; they don't work so hard. They gonna die soon anyway." Then, very quick, he take the ax and hit them in the back of the head. Blood fly everywhere. The wall of the temple, beautiful tile, beautiful painting, now all dripping with blood. . . . Then the Khmer Rouge says to us, "It's time for your job. You pee on them. You pee on their head." I think: I will not do this terrible thing, I will not do this . . . But then I look down, and I see the urine coming out of me.
>
> (101)

It is gut wrenching for any reader. In my view, the text resists sentimentality in its abrupt phrasing, declarative sentence structure, and present tense, mimicking the way that the survivors had to act swiftly and resist emotion in order to survive. The effect is a body detached from the mind as though Arn is a ghost detached from his Khmer body.

But Arn is not a ghost, and while he has "acted tough" to survive, McCormick's authorial strategy is to then juxtapose the haunting automaticity of terror with Arn's humanity. Arn is called to a leader's home to play music and later asked to ride a horse to deliver a letter:

> Strange thing is happening now. Nice thing. But very strange. Smile on my face. Not fake smile like when we sing song about Angkar, but real smile, and laughing. Also wetness on my cheek like rain, but it's tear. For three years, laughing not allowed, crying not allowed. Now, on this horse, I am laughing so much I am also crying.
>
> (106)

This juxtaposition of images and McCormick's attention to syntax is something that only an artist can do. In "Author's Note," McCormick talks about her in-depth interviews with the people for whom the characters were named and from whom the novel derived. She says that she crafted a novel from her interviews because of the gaps in the memories of the participants in her research. And she explains that she wrote the character using

Arn's "own distinct and beautiful voice" to make up for the "light" lost with grammar and syntax. McCormick's recreation of Arn's voice is unfamiliar syntactically and immediate temporally because it is in present tense. I think this shows what Gallagher finds compelling about the novel, that the novel considers the reader "external to the fiction and capable of speculating on the action," and in doing so, "the novel seeks to suspend such disbelief" yet not going so far as to ask the reader to believe (348).

As a fiction writer, McCormick could have wrapped up this novel with a happy ending in which Arn makes it to Thailand safely and finds the American dream awaiting him; she doesn't, and I think this authorial decision is an ethical appeal. Yes, it is a miracle that Arn made it to the Thailand refugee camp (as did other survivors), but his story of genocide did not end there. McCormick further complicates the "neat" storytelling of children's literature (i.e., happy endings). Surviving mass murder was not the end of the story for McCormick's protagonist or for survivors of genocide. They must survive their survival. In some novels about genocide, the character survives, the reader experiences relief, and the book is closed. Instead, Arn's ethical appeal is strengthened by troubling the reader's understanding of survival and genocide—neither is an event that ends. The day-to-day struggle of coping with the past, facing the present, and imagining a future is complex, and to represent it otherwise is unjust and an insult to the reader.

Arn makes it to America—New Hampshire—with Reverend Peter Pond (who later adopted him and sixteen other Cambodian children) and begins high school only to face the challenges of learning a new culture and language and unlearning the "tough act" that became his best survival tool. Here Arn is telling his readers about learning English with his "special teacher":

> Very important sound this th. But we don't have this sound in Khmer. So my tongue can't do it. But Pat, she say it over and over and over. Get close to my face, closer and closer she get; her tongue, she show it to me, pushing on her teeth, like she gonna eat me. And I spit her. Right in the face, I spit. . . . And I think: why I spit at this person, only one trying to help me? Why I'm so bad? Why?
>
> (196)

I am not sure what Wendy Hesford would say about this humanitarian narrative—that Arn was "saved" by a Western figure. It does not weaken the novel, however; indeed, it is plausible (and true in some cases). While humanitarian interventions perhaps save the body, they cannot save the mind or the mind imagines its existence. In the end, Arn says:

> My heart like, like a tiger inside, clawing my rib to get out. So much hate in there it hurt. Hate for the people who kill my family, hate for the

> people who kill my friend, hate for myself. . . . "Why I live?" I ask Peter. "Why I live and so many people die?"
>
> (207)

Arn saves himself by surviving the Khmer Rouge and by getting Peter Pond to select him from all the children in the camp. It is the act of finding his voice that really saves him. It is Arn's ability to lay down thoughts of violence—against himself, his adoptive brother, his classmates—that transforms him.

A note from Patricia McCormick about writing genocide literature:

> Just because the subject matter is brutal, you don't have to brutalize the reader. If a young reader is going to follow my characters through harrowing situations, I make sure that as the "tour guide," I am as gentle and thoughtful as I can be. I make very careful choices with the language and point of view employed by a child narrator. You won't find graphic language, per se, in my books: that's because the main character isn't going to express his/her experience with what we would call "graphic language." The young protagonist is going to describe the experience in terms of bewilderment, confusion, betrayal and a slowing dawning realization of the precariousness of her situation. That, to me, is far more poignant—and therefore more powerful than any graphic language would convey.

Conclusion

The aesthetic of fiction is its plausibility, but in order to draw readers into the imaginary plane of the novel, the author must establish credibility. For McCormick, this meant making an ethical appeal to readers through and with her narrator. The rhetorical effect of Arn's child narratorial voice aligned the reader much like a witness in testimonial literature uncovering the context as he observed it and unveiling the darkest deeds of humanity as he experienced it. At no point does the narrator comfort his readers or attempt to offer any rationale for that which he witnessed; to do so would undermine his ethical appeal as an observant, bewildered child. And yet the aesthetic of fiction cannot position readers as witnesses; its task is to make conscious in the readers' imagination a world where this can and did happen.

Works Cited

Gallagher, Catherine. "The Rise of Fictionality." Ed. Franco Moretti. *The Novel: History, Geography, and Culture.* Princeton: Princeton University Press, 2006. 336–363. Print.

Genette, Gérard, and Jane E. Lewin. *Narrative Discourse Revisited*. Ithaca, NY: Cornell University Press, 1988. Print.

Gilbert, Ruth. "Grasping the Unimaginable: Recent Holocaust Novels for Children by Morris Gleitzman and John Boyne." *Children's Literature in Education*. 41.4 (2010): 355–366. Web.

Hesford, Wendy S. *Spectacular Rhetorics: Human Rights Visions, Recognitions, Feminisms.* Durham, NC: Duke University Press, 2011. Print.
Jordan, Sarah D. "Educating Without Overwhelming Authorial Strategies in Children's Holocaust Literature." *Children's Literature in Education.* 35.3 (2004): 199–218. Print.
Mannix, Patrick. *The Rhetoric of Antinuclear Fiction: Persuasive Strategies in Novels and Films.* Lewisburg, PA: Bucknell University Press, 1992. Print.
McCormick, Patricia. *Never Fall Down: A Boy Soldier's Story of Survival.* New York: Balzer, 2012. Print.
———. "Re: Never Fall Down." *Message to Sarah Donovan.* 11 Nov. 2014. Email.

Literature for Your Classroom Library, Cambodia

Baillie, Allan. *Little Brother.* New York: Viking, 1992. Print.
Crew, Linda. *Children of the River.* New York: Delacorte Press, 1989. Print.
Ho, Minfong. *The Clay Marble.* New York: Farrar, Straus, Giroux, 1991. Print.
Ho, Minfong. *The Stone Goddess.* New York: Orchard Books, 2003. Print.
Ratner, Vaddey. *In the Shadow of the Banyan.* New York: Simon & Schuster, 2012. Print.
Smith, Icy, and Sopaul Nhem. *Half Spoon of Rice: A Survival Story of the Cambodian Genocide.* Manhattan Beach, CA: East West Discovery Press, 2010. Print.

7 Emotional Appeals, Trauma, and Aesthetic Pleasure

Why read literature? Most theories of literary criticism maintain that at least part of the purpose of literature is the stimulation of pleasure. While the source and the importance of this pleasure vary, the insistence on the pleasurable emotion seems universal. According to Patrick Mannix, author of *The Rhetoric of Antinuclear Fiction: Persuasive Strategies in Novels and Films*, what the rhetoricality of fiction does is to attempt to use the aesthetic "pleasure" of the work to help cultivate the reader's allegiance to some thematic point (118). Emotional appeals persuade the audience by arousing emotions and passions within the audience to move them to act (Corbett 319). Emotional appeals, then, endeavor to produce an aesthetic "pleasure" in the reader that is as enlivening and enlightening.

Such a word "pleasure" in a book about genocide may seem grotesque. As readers of genocide literature, we might feel it is wrong to find pleasure in an image of suffering; it should feel wrong to want to look at the suffering such as the example of the image in *Never Fall Down* of a child soldier feeding on a corpse. Such pleasure is "unwanted," yet it is an essential element of aesthetic genres. The "unwanted beauty," as discussed in Brett Kaplan's *Unwanted Beauty: Aesthetic Pleasure in Holocaust Representation*, is a beauty that is also mournful; it entices our "reflection, our attention, and our questioning" (1). Indeed, pleasure and ethics are entwined, yet pleasure is more subjective, transactional (i.e., dependent on the reader–text transaction). In the aesthetic transaction, what is this pleasure a reader experiences? A catharsis? An "illicit pleasure"? Is it exploitative? Whether or not one agrees that persuasion is a valid *purpose* of fiction, authors of aesthetic genres like novels *do* persuade, *do* move their readers, and they do so by attending to aesthetic pleasure (Mannix). By entering into this persuasive process, fiction facilitates the communication of history to mass audiences, perhaps tempering the lessons with the aesthetic pleasure.

The emotional appeal of beauty comes from evoking the ambiguity, complexity, nuance, and even incompleteness in the subject, characters, or landscape. The aesthetic of fiction, again its plausibility, moves the reader to rethink, reflect, and ponder. Readers walk away from the text with more questions than answers, prompting some transformation or agency (thus, the rhetorical nature of aesthetics). A large part of the artist's purpose, then, is to communicate some point about human life in the hopes of winning or reinforcing the audience's allegiance to the point; at the same time each work attempts to give the audience the aesthetic pleasure that distinguishes literature from other forms of communication like informational texts.

Artists represent subjects so as to evoke an emotional response and thus allegiance to a conceptual idea. Technologically, the writer is bringing the reader into a position to bear witness. Unlike social media and television (and some informational texts), young-adult genocide novels call attention to fictionality, which makes clear to the reader that the events depicted are, indeed, representations. The artist-author, however, does not merely reproduce events to "tell" a young reader what happened; they must imagine it so that their readers can also imagine. The literature, as a work of art, supports the realization of the events in our consciousness. The imaginative medium of the novel (not the testimony of an actual genocide survivor but an artist rendering the experience) has the task of opening up in the reader the "imaginative capability of perceiving history—what is happening to others—*in one's own body*, with the power of sight (of insight) usually afforded only by one's own immediate physical involvement" (Felman and Laub 108). It is the task of the young-adult author to make this experience accessible to her teen readers without losing the aesthetic; otherwise, the account would be in a textbook and the "lived-through" experience would be lost (Rosenblatt). Young-adult authors make emotional appeals to their readers all the time, but in genocide novels, there are ethical implications for attempting to get young readers to embody what is happening to others in genocide. Let us now consider how one author negotiated the dilemma of making emotional appeals in genocide fiction.

Published in 1999, *The Hunger* by Marsha Forchuk Skrypuch is a novel about the Turkish massacre of Armenians that is still not publicly defined as genocide in Turkey. *The Hunger* is a story of personal and historical trauma; however, Skrypuch creates an element of split subjectivity when Paula, the protagonist living in the early twentieth century and suffering from anorexia, enters a comatose state. While in a coma, Paula embodies her own great-grandmother Marta in the year 1915 as she (Paula-Marta) is being deported into the Syrian Desert. Having done some research on the Armenian deportations for a school project prior to her coma, Paula's altered consciousness permits her to invent the deportation scene, but the storyteller, Skrypuch, imagines for Paula that which is unimaginable. Paula witnesses, firsthand, Marta's escape from deportation and years living in a harem, experiences that include rape by her "husband" (though not depicted) and enslavement by the first wife.

In the following passage, Paula is coming out of her coma as the split subject of Marta/Paula unified. What Marta sees in the future is an image of emaciation, but the scarred knuckles indicate evidence of her (Paula's) trauma of self-imposed starvation:

> There stood an emaciated woman [Paula] wrapped in a stiff white sheet. Marta's throat filled with tears when she regarded the woman's hollow eyes and sunken cheeks. This woman had suffered through famine and ravages too. Marta reached out to touch the woman's hand—to give comfort. Then she noticed the scars on the knuckles and the needle marks on her arm. With a start, she understood that this was Paula. Marta's heart was filled with sorrow . . . And then Marta no longer existed. She had stepped inside Paula.
>
> (*The Hunger* 157)

The split subjectivity positions Paula as the secondhand witness (the body is Paula's) *and* Marta the firsthand witness (the memory is Marta's) simultaneously. The images of "scars on the knuckles" and "needle marks on the arm" are emotional appeals to the teen reader with potentially familiar markers of anorexia (which begins with personal agency for the victim), yet the self-inflicted starvation is represented as analogous to the "hollow eyes" and "sunken cheeks" of state-inflicted starvation (that which is perpetrated). In my view, as a testimony to the personal trauma of anorexia, *The Hunger* works; literature is a mode of "truth's realization beyond what is available as statement, beyond what is known" (Felman 15–16). However, Skrypuch's representation of Marta's trauma is problematic; the emotional appeal to readers is *for* Paula and not Marta, a human rights subject. The human rights violation, the historical trauma of the Turkish genocide of Armenians from 1915 to 1923, is minimized in an attempt to align the teenaged Paula to the teenaged reader.

The Hunger is a novel that an English teacher might teach in a middle or high school class for the purpose of meeting the genocide education mandate or "covering" a topic like anorexia or war. A teacher might recognize that identity and body image are relevant to adolescents' lives and that this novel might work on personal, familial, and perhaps international levels. However, it is also important to consider how the text imagines genocide and how it implicates the reader in the spectacle of analogous traumas (anorexia and genocide-induced starvation)? In my view, the split subjectivity in *The Hunger* illuminates the important limitation of the secondhand witness. Bearing witness is a critical stance wherein the witness *does not* take the place of the other. According to Hesford, the risk in representing trauma and violence is "the impossibility of empathetic merging" (99). Skrypuch's authorial strategy of split subjectivity illuminates this risk by making anorexia analogous to forced starvation. On one hand, this can be read as the possibility of empathic merging. Readers might be manipulated into thinking they can imaginatively embody another person's trauma. On the other hand, readers may see Skrypuch as attempting to show the failed merging of Paula's scarred hands with Marta's hollowed eyes; the rhetorical effect is an emotional appeal to personal and historical trauma that cannot reach empathy. In my view, sympathy is the best we can do as readers and witnesses to one another's lives. In this way, *The Hunger* undermines easy notions of empathy. The empathy a teen reader might feel when identifying with the teen protagonist's struggle for self-worth cannot be transferred so easily to a human rights subject. How can one imagine or empathize with the trauma of genocide having not lived through it? (While I believe literature can cultivate a capacity for empathy, in my view and with regard to genocide literature, I find empathy perhaps too presumptuous.)

The emotional appeal can have varied consequences in young-adult genocide novels: from pity to responsibility to rejection. If the reader is moved to feel pity, she may experience what Arabella Lyon identifies in "Misrepresentations of Missing Women in the U.S. Press: The Rhetorical Uses of Disgust, Pity, and Compassion" as Aristotelian pity: "They come to feel the character's pain, see the characters' conditions as possible for them, and achieve the closeness of time and space that is required for an educated emotional response" (188). Nevertheless, Lyon would suggest this response could be seen as a sort of failure in recognition in that the reader's response to the novel is "isolated from spaces that would allow a productive discussion of human rights" (188). Lyon explains that the reader is caught up in pity and does not recognize the larger political and global processes that made genocide and human rights violations possible.

A note from the author, Marsha Skrypuch:

> *The Hunger* was published at a time that no one was writing or publishing fiction about the Armenian Genocide, and really, about no genocide at all except the Holocaust. I had tried to find a publisher for a completely historical novel set during the Armenian Genocide, but it was not possible. My agent was continually told that such a novel would find no readership. The only reason I could get away with writing about the Armenian Genocide at all was because I rewrote it and framed it into a novel about an eating disorder. It wasn't until the 9/11 tragedy that YA publishers and commercial publishers understood there was a market for serious history, and in particular untold aspects of history. It is somewhat unfair to judge *The Hunger* by the same standards as one might hold other genocide novels. *The Hunger* broke new ground at a time when most YA fiction was fluff, and it made way for later novels on the same subject.

Conclusion

Perhaps at minimum, what we can hope from the ethical appeal in a young-adult genocide novel is that it frames one way of understanding genocide and gives readers a situation for deliberation. At best, we can hope that the reader understands the human rights subject as having agency, as being part of what Hesford describes as "a heterogeneous and [as] a rhetorically dialogic process," and the reader, as an actor in the process, will act more justly (19). In this sense, the character in the novel becomes a rights-bearing subject whose life has been shaped by social and economic conditions and who possesses agency (57). Perhaps the narrative can resist victimizing the victim by complicating rescue narratives or transformation narratives. A clever author can help teen readers be skeptical of images and see human rights subjects as "complex subjects whose subjectivity is not grounded in a struggle for recognition but in their ability to respond to impoverished, social and economic circumstances"(182). Even if the authors of young-adult genocide novels cannot achieve this, readers can learn to recognize emotional appeals and deliberate, together, the ethics of such appeals.

Works Cited

Corbett, Edward. *Classical Rhetoric for Modern Students*. New York: Oxford University Press, 1971. Print.

Hesford, Wendy S. *Spectacular Rhetorics: Human Rights Visions, Recognitions, Feminisms*. Durham, NC: Duke University Press, 2011. Print.

Kaplan, Brett Ashley. *Unwanted Beauty: Aesthetic Pleasure in Holocaust Representation*. Urbana: University of Illinois, 2007. Print.

Lyon, Arabella. "Misrepresentations of Missing Women in the U.S. Press: The Rhetorical Uses of Disgust, Pity, and Compassion." Ed. Wendy Hesford and Wendy Kozol. *Just Advocacy? Women's Human Rights, Transnational Feminisms, and the Politics of Representation*. New Brunswick: Rutgers University Press, 2005. 172–194. Print.

Mannix, Patrick. *The Rhetoric of Antinuclear Fiction: Persuasive Strategies in Novels and Films*. Lewisburg, PA: Bucknell University Press, 1992. Print.

Rosenblatt, Louise. *Literature as Exploration*. New York: Appleton Century, 1938. 4th ed. New York: Modern Language Association, 1983. Print.

Skrypuch, Marsha Forchuk. *The Hunger*. Toronto: Dundurn Group, 1999. Print.

———. "RE: The Hunger." *Message to Sarah Donovan*. 15 Feb. 2016. Email.

8 Rational Appeals and Didacticism

For the ancient Greeks, rational appeal or *logos* means "thought plus action" (Covino and Jolliffe 17). The ideas are the "thought," and the way those ideas are presented to the audience is the "action." When I talk about rational appeal in genocide fiction, I am not only referring to the logic of the plot but to the methods of presentation so that readers are more likely to accept the plausibility of the narrative; thus, I am referring to *how* the information about genocide is presented. We tend to think of fiction as a representation of imaginary actions that exist in their own self-contained world. We do not normally expect the author to stop in the middle of relating a story to tell us historical information or explain the context. And yet if the action of the novel, play, or film revolves around some complex issue like genocide, the author will find a way to include in her fictional action a representation of the precipitating events, social and cultural issues, motives, consequences, and lessons (Mannix 73). When the "information" of it all is too obvious, however, novels can be accused of being too didactic, and so our consideration as English teachers reading genocide novels alongside our students is how authors maintain the aesthetic of fiction *and* make rational appeals.

Didacticism is the instructional quality of something, but extreme forms of intellectually controlled fiction related to the real world can be called "didactic." Allegory and satire are didactic forms of texts; in these genres, readers accept that there is some sort of lesson to be gleaned from the story. Scholes et al., in *The Nature of Narrative*, explain that the word "didactic" tends to inhibit discussions of fictional works in which intellectual considerations influence narrative structure. "Didactic" is typically used in a pejorative sense: "We are likely to think of a 'didactic' narrative as one in which a feeble attempt is made to clothe ethical chestnuts in fictional form, resulting at best in a spoiled story" (106). They suggest that we "strip the word of its negative connotations" and allow the word to refer to a work "which emphasizes the intellectual and instructional potential of narrative" (106). Scholes et al. note many didactic authors—Aesop, Dante, Milton, Swift, George Eliot, Lawrence, and Proust—whose works "put to the most strenuous kind of examination the most problematic and profound ethical and metaphysical questions" (106). When it comes to genocide fiction for young adults, authors must examine the complexity of the genocide process, which includes historical, social, political, economic, and environmental tensions of the context and the ethical questions among these tensions.

According to Patrick Mannix, who considers the persuasive strategies in antinuclear fiction, there are at least two strategies authors can use to insert factual information into fiction. The narrator can introduce the facts as needed, or characters can include specifics as part of the dialogue. "In the first instance," Mannix suggests, "he must be careful not to let his novel degenerate into a contrived fact book" (74). Indeed, such is considered didactic literature (of which students are suspicious). Mannix seems to prefer the second, as it makes "the exposition flow naturally or at least as naturally as exposition normally flows" (74). Wayne Booth in *The Rhetoric of Fiction* suggests this is the difference between direct and authoritative rhetoric. If the story is presented without comment, it leaves the reader without guidance of explicit evaluation, but the author's voice in fiction, if engaged fully, has aesthetic implications. Of course, it is economical for the author to impose virtues on the reader, to simply tell and then support the telling with detail, but this would result in an aesthetic failure. However, Booth suggests that everything the author *shows* will serve to tell; the author's judgment is always present, always evident to anyone who knows to look for it (17).

Fiction writers make rational appeals by going "behind" to reveal true workings of the character's mind and heart or through overt action (Booth); those are rational appeals, mechanisms for telling information. To avoid aesthetic failure, then, the author must manipulate the tale in such a way as to make the reader desire such an effect (e.g., an inner monologue, another point of view, a description of such and such a place, a little historical note, etc.). Didacticism, then, is less didactic when the reader is left wanting.

To consider rational appeals and the art of didacticism, I want to take a look at one of Marsha Forchuk Skrypuch's follow-up novels to *The Hunger: Daughter of War*. Unlike *The Hunger* (1999), *Daughter of War* (2008) was published at a time when there was a market for "serious history, and in particular untold aspects of history" (Skrypuch email). Indeed, the publishing date is post-9/11, but it is also post-Colin Powell's naming of Darfur as genocide. In his testimony before the Senate Foreign Relations Committee on September 9, 2004, Powell stated:

> Some seem to have been waiting for this determination of genocide to take action. In fact, however, no new action is dictated by this determination. We have been doing everything we can to get the Sudanese Government to act responsibly. So let us not be too preoccupied with this designation. These people are in desperate need and we must help them. Call it civil war; call it ethnic cleansing; call it genocide; call it "none of the above." The reality is the same. There are people in Darfur who desperately need the help of the international community.

Skrypuch's *Daughter of War* did not need to be "framed"; people were and still are "preoccupied with this designation" of the word "genocide."

Skrypuch introduces factual information about the Armenian Genocide through textual features that are external to the narrative: maps with descriptors that provide a chronology of events and a historical note. Readers will see the helpful map with the routes of several characters carefully indicated along with the various concentration camps in Turkey and Syria. Skrypuch also includes a helpful "Historical Note" to tell readers about the Muslims and Arabs who rescued Armenians (e.g., raising child survivors as Muslims, taking women in as concubines or slaves, and disguising some survivors as nomadic Arabs). Elizabeth Baer, in "A New Algorithm in Evil: Children's Literature in a Post-Holocaust World," suggests such features like maps and historical notes provide a wider context for readers that is not intrusive or disruptive to the narrative, thus preserving the novel's aesthetic. However, Mannix and Booth would likely say such addendums are overtly didactic and compromise the aesthetic value of the text as a whole. In other words, while maps, notes, and other external features like glossaries and pictures may function as rational appeals, they may detract from the aesthetic of fiction. In borrowing informational text features, the imaginative appeal of fiction might be compromised.

Next, when including information about victims, perpetrators, bystanders, and rescuers, authors must attend to the circumstances that encouraged or discouraged individuals' choices and actions. Fiction authors provide an imaginative opportunity for readers to grapple with the challenge of thinking about the interiority and motivations of historical actors. If the novel can capture the complexity of the human conscience, then readers just might be less likely to build stereotypical views of human rights actors (e.g., victim, bystander, perpetrator, and rescuer). In *Daughter of War*, Skrypuch makes central the choices and experiences of different Armenian and Muslim characters to illustrate the disparate motives and values of individuals living in the Ottoman Empire. As indicated in "Historical Note" and depicted in the novel, in 1915, as Armenians were marched into the Syrian Desert without food or water under the guise of "relocation," Muslim families rescued many Armenian children and raised them as Muslims. Still, some young Armenian women were "rescued" from death marches to serve as concubines or slaves. And still other Armenians were rescued by nomadic Arabs and taught an Arab way of life to survive persecution. In the novel, Marta and Mariam are Armenian sisters rescued by Turks, and Kevork is an Armenian rescued by an Arab clan. After they were rescued, Marta, Mariam, and Kevork had to learn how to live in duplicity. Skrypuch's task is to invite readers into the conscience of these characters, as their circumstances pose ethical dilemmas. Skrypuch's omniscient narrator makes readers privy to the minds and actions of these characters, and as they negotiate their mental and physical survival, readers contemplate the meaning of *good* and *right* when it comes to survival. For example, Marta, rescued to serve as a concubine, becomes pregnant by her captor. The captor's first wife, Idris, has not been able to give her husband a son and worries that Marta will give birth to a son and replace her as first wife. Both Marta and Idris have to negotiate the dynamics of their complex relationship. Once rescued, how does one survive as the rescued and the rescuer? There are no clear answers or easy logic to negotiate such complexity. Thus, Skrypuch crafts an imaginative truth in this passage as Idris helps Marta off the back of the cart:

> Marta was struck by her [Idris's] demeanor . . ., but there was no need for duplicity here. Did this mean that Idris was actually starting to miss her? More than likely, it was all the housecleaning Idris would miss. No, Marta thought again, that was being unfair. Idris did not have to go through so much trouble to get rid of her. Marta owed this woman her life.
>
> (*Daughter of War* 28)

In this short passage, young readers will not see an overly optimistic view of human nature but rather a framework for response. Reading ethically here, as with witnessing, means considering multiple points of view, including the circumstances, choices, and logic that guide the actions of others. What is *right* and who is *good* can often be quite ambiguous. The rhetorical effect of self-disguise, in my view, is that the novel explores what it might have been like to live with this uncertainty of discovery and ambivalence of identity. At the center of the plot, then, is the complexity of individual agency within the site of genocide. However, Skrypuch does address international actors.

In a novel that commemorates the resilience of Armenians, Western readers may be left wondering about the international community, international rescuers: *Didn't anyone try to stop it?* In this sense, Skrypuch's novel functions as an agent of memory taking up the task of remembering and accounting for "what happened." What *Daughter of War* does well, and this speaks to its rational appeal in providing a wider context, is how it captures the transnational nature of genocide. In most instances of genocide, actors within the international community can be identified within genocidal processes. For example, in Rwanda, China sold the Hutus machetes used to massacre Tutsis, and French troops helped the Hutu regime flee the country. In the case of Armenia, in 1915, Great Britain, France, and Russia identified the Young Turks as responsible for crimes against humanity. Allied forces sent humanitarian aid to save the starving Armenians, and American, British, and German governments sponsored efforts to report the atrocities. Nevertheless, according to the Armenian National Institute, "no actions were taken against the Ottoman Empire either to sanction its brutal policies or to salvage the Armenian people from the grip of extermination."

In *Daughter of War*, Skrypuch had to find a way to include the failure of the international community without "degenerating into a contrived fact book" (Mannix). While Skrypuch's main characters are fictional, she makes one exception, and, in my view, her authorial choice works to represent and implicate the international community in genocide. Skrypuch's novel breaks the imaginative plane by including an actual historical actor. In the Historical Note, she writes,

> The characters are fictionalized with the exception of Leslie A. Davis, who was an American consul. His observations were published in 1989 in his first-hand observations of the Armenian genocide in *The Slaughterhouse Province: An American Diplomat's Report on the Armenian Genocide: 1915–1917.*

In the novel, Davis's character offers a glimpse of the international context and international response to the atrocities, which suggests that Turkey's crimes were systematic, transnational, and not strictly ethnically motivated. While this novel does not explicitly uncover the Young Turks' political or economic motives, readers note America's awareness of the atrocities and its attempts to *furtively* organize humanitarian aid for the camps and provide safe houses to organize deportations. (To be clear, there was no public, organized effort to intervene.) The covert efforts, however, put some Armenians in further danger. This "information" is embedded in the plot, and Kevork's character illustrates the reasoning and choice of one Armenian to help the Americans. After a forced march into the desert, Kevork was rescued by an Arab clan and taught to live as an Arab to hide from the Turks. Readers meet Kevork at the beginning of the novel in Aleppo, Syria, working as an Arab shoemaker, and he later accepts work as a courier for the Americans. Because he is an Armenian, the Americans can trust him, and because he looks like an Arab, he can safely transport payments for safe houses and deportations. Kevork's motivation to help the Americans, however, is not cultural pride; it is to look for his betrothed, Marta, in the camps. The Americans, however, intentionally foil his labors because as a courier, he is valuable to their refugee mission. For example, Kevork wants the Americans to send a message to the orphanage to see if Marta is alive, but the Americans are faced with a dilemma:

> In her [Miss Schultz's] heart, she knew that the right thing to do was to send this telegraph. But John Coren had warned her that Kevork might ask this of her. He told her that under no circumstances should she send the message on. He explained that they needed Kevork's talent as a courier. What would happen to the thousands of starving Armenians if Kevork ran off to find his Marta? Wasn't humanity best served if he thought her dead?
>
> (73)

In this passage, we can see the ethical, emotional, and rational appeals of the narrative. The rescue narrative, so familiar to young readers, presents the humanitarian logic of the powerful West saving victims while inducing the reader to feel pity for Kevork and also Miss Schultz (Davis's assistant). There is even this sense that we are witnessing a mode of modernity, as Coren (Davis's courier) has to covertly provide humanitarian aid because the international community is not publicly intervening.

Authorial technique is rhetorical in that readers can see what an author is willing to do in order to do justice to reality, be true to life, and be intensely alive (Booth 37). More importantly, and this is why young-adult genocide fiction is our subject, "accurate transcription of actuality does not easily produce a work of any real truth" (41). The rhetoricality of the fiction, then, is in service of realism. Nevertheless, as Gallagher points out, once the novelist has done his job, the reader pulls together what the novelist presents: the scenes, gestures, dramatized comments, and omniscient judgment. The text works upon the reader and the reader works upon the text in a transactional process to make meaning, but at no point, and this is reiterated by Booth, does the reader pretend that she is not reading a novel (53).

Conclusion

Like eighteenth-century novelists, some twentieth- and twenty-first-century novelists have taken up the task of writing genocide novels to expose the darker side of modernity and how interests in technological, economic, cultural and political advancement have led to crimes against humanity (Mignolo). As Gallagher writes, "[A]lmost all the developments we associate with modernity—from greater religious toleration to specific scientific discovery—required the kind of cognitive provisionality one practices in reading fiction, a competence in investing contingent and temporary credit" (347). And so we might see fiction's aesthetic of plausibility as doing that which nonfiction cannot. The novel represents not only what has been reported as real but that which is beyond knowing yet plausible. Fiction creates distance from reality while inviting a temporary suspension of disbelief so that we can, in fact, build some sort of capacity for considering how society *is* beyond our experience of it and how society *ought* to be.

Genocide novels illuminate the author's ethical responsibility in representing human rights violations and the reader's epistemological and ethical responsibilities in negotiating history and imagination. In creating her art, the artist-author is faced with the concerns put forth by Kertesz, Levi, Lang, Trezise, Adorno, and Wiesel regarding the "barbaric" act of representing the most horrific acts of humankind. Readers feel the ethical dilemmas of expressing human rights violations through language as the page confronts their own sense of our civilization. However, unless the English classroom calls attention to students' agency in the transactional reading process and the rhetoricality of the text, the ethical reasoning that fiction offers can be lost. To be clear, I am suggesting the aesthetic of fiction negotiates fact and deception through its aesthetic of plausibility above reality and that the novel is a framework for ethical reasoning. In order to uncover the benefits of the aesthetic of fiction in novels, however, we must teach students to read a novel rhetorically, i.e., to read for ethical, emotional, and rational appeals. How does the artist earn trust from her readers and establish credibility in this realm of fiction? How does she make emotional appeals while representing genocide? Finally, how does she treat the didactic and "rational" details of that genocide?

Works Cited

Baer, Elizabeth. "A New Algorithm in Evil—Children's Literature in a Post-Holocaust World." *The Lion and the Unicorn.* 24.3 (2000): 378–401. Web.

Booth, Wayne C. *The Rhetoric of Fiction.* Chicago: University of Chicago, 1961. Print.

Covino, William, and David Jolliffe. *Rhetoric: Concepts, Definitions, Boundaries.* Boston: Allyn and Bacon, 1995. Print.

"Frequently Asked Questions About the Armenian Genocide." *Armenian National Institute.* 15 May 2016. Web.

Gallagher, Catherine. "The Rise of Fictionality." Ed. Franco Moretti. *The Novel: History, Geography, and Culture.* Princeton, NJ: Princeton University Press, 2006. 336–63. Print.

Mannix, Patrick. *The Rhetoric of Antinuclear Fiction: Persuasive Strategies in Novels and Films.* Lewisburg, PA: Bucknell University Press, 1992. Print.

Mignolo, Walter D. *The Darker Side of Western Modernity: Global Futures, Decolonial Options.* Durham, NC: Duke University Press, 2011. Print.

Powell, Colin. "The Crisis in Darfur: Testimony Before the Senate Foreign Relations Committee." *U.S. Department of State: Archive.* 9 Sept. 2004. Web.

Scholes, Robert, James Phelan, and Robert Kellogg. *The Nature of Narrative: Revised and Expanded.* Oxford: Oxford Press, 2006. Print.

Skrypuch, Marsha Forchuk. *Daughter of War: A Novel.* Markham, ONT: Fitzhenry & Whiteside, 2008. Print.

———. *The Hunger.* Toronto: Dundurn Group, 1999. Print.

———. "RE: The Hunger." *Message to Sarah Donovan.* 15 Feb. 2015. Email.

Literature for Your Classroom Library, Armenian Genocide

Bagdasarian, Adam. *Forgotten Fire.* New York: Laurel-Leaf, 2002. Print.

Bohjalian, Chris. *The Sandcastle Girls: A Novel,* 2012. Print.

Skrypuch, Marsha F. *Nobody's Child.* Toronto: Boardwalk Books, 2003. Print.

Walrath, Dana. *Like Water on Stone.* New York: Delacorte Press, 2014. Print.

Part IV

Into the Classroom

9 The Writing Workshop

What are ways to help students read testimonial texts meaningfully, to explore how and why they were written, to recognize in them expressions and articulations of the human condition that are relevant to their own lives, and to find in them enriched understandings of injustice and alienation that prompt them to action? One way might be to draw upon *writing* testimonial texts to teach students the *process* and *experience* of writing testimonial texts. Donald Graves (1983) inspired many teachers to make writer's workshop a part of the English classroom, and the work of others like Donald Murray (1985), Lucy Calkins (1986), and Nancie Atwell (1987) has supported K–12 writing workshop over the years. Process-oriented classrooms recognize that when writers work through the stages of writing (e.g., prewriting, drafting, revising, conferencing, revising again, and editing for publication), they are working through questions that they need to answer for themselves and for readers (Dutro and McIver 94). The writing–reading relationship, then, has potential to support students in their writing practice and their reading practice.

To prepare students to write or to support students during the writing process, teachers might bring in "mentor texts," or exemplars in a specific genre, so that students have examples of the genre's text structure or an author's techniques (Dutro and McIver). In writing, mentor texts are in the service of writing practice. While I do think (and will show in what follows) that the process of writing a personal narrative can nurture and support the ethical practice of witnessing and prepare students to read genocide literature with greater consciousness of their role in that reading–writing relationship, I do not think genocide testimonial literature should be used as mentor texts. In the case of genocide literature, we would want to avoid students reading a genocide testimony as a tool for problem solving their own memoir, just as we would want to avoid asking a student to imagine a genocide situation (or some simulation) in order to prepare them to read. According to Totten, "The activity may engage students, but they often forget the purpose of the lesson, and even worse, they are left with the impression at the conclusion of the activity that they now know what it [genocide] was like" (18). Instead, I suggest that the process of writing a personal narrative has the potential for building a capacity for witnessing and deterring indifference.

Testimonial literature has an important purpose in the modern English classroom. Through witnessing, students learn to attend to others, but what of all those stories without witnesses, stories to which our students do not have access? Consider all the voices that remain silent, all the accounts of the human experience hidden by oppressive institutions and beliefs that perpetuate injustice and violence in the world. One way our students can gain access to those hidden experiences of humankind and contemplate what their society *ought* to be is by developing their conscious imagination.

In thinking about how to nurture and support witnessing in my own classroom and before witnessing the testimony of a genocide survivor, I wanted students to practice witnessing, writing testimony, sharing the testimony, and listening-bearing witness to the testimony of others. I realize that most English teachers do not teach solely reading and literature any more than they just teach composition. Most of us have about fifty minutes a day with students to teach *all* that is English (reading, literature, vocabulary, grammar, composition, speaking, listening, etc.). During the 2012–2013 school year, I was fortunate to have a double block, eighty minutes, with a group of about thirty eighth graders, to teach "all that is English." And so in this section I invite readers to bear witness in my classroom as I put into practice the process of witnessing. You will hopefully notice all the experiences that have shaped me and continue to shape me as a human being and inform my practice and choices as a teacher: my own life experiences, authors, scholars, professional development, travel, reading experiences, writing experiences, and certainly, students.

A few weeks before we read *First They Killed My Father*, a memoir about the genocide carried out by Pol Pot and his Khmer Rouge regime between 1975 and 1979 in Cambodia, we began writing personal narratives during writing workshop time, which was usually the second half of the block. During writing workshop, I wanted to call attention to the partial-ness of narrative, how despite all our efforts, any story we wrote would leave gaps, and perhaps those gaps are what make narrative so intriguing. I had spent a decade practicing the lessons of writing pedagogy experts like Nancie Atwell, Donald Graves, and Donald Murray, and I think I had done a fairly good job of honoring their student-oriented pedagogy. During that school year, however, I had read another text on writing during a graduate course at the University of Illinois at Chicago (UIC): *Writing as a Way of Being* (2011) by Robert Yagelski. Yagelski offered an ontological argument about writing with others that moved me to recognize that my focus on the writer and the writing product blinded me to the potential of focusing on the actual writing experience. And when I became conscious of this, when I focused on the experience of witnessing my life with writing, I recognized how writing was witnessing. Through the activity of writing, we are witnessing our lives.

In *Writing as a Way of Being*, Yagelski explores what anyone who has ever written something they believe at the time to be important already knows: the actual experience of writing is quite separate from the text. And this is why once the piece of text is "finished," a writer may feel distanced from the memory, I would go so far as to say somewhat melancholy, realizing that the "finishing" of the text was nowhere near as exhilarating as the writing itself. As Young indicates, "the writer and link to events may thus be reified not in the writer's words, but in the writing activity that brought words to the page" (420). The writing activity, then, is the remembering (if not reliving) and the translating of the occurrence across time and space. When the writing stops, so too does the occurrence.

When teachers talk about writing as having the potential to change the world, admittedly a lofty goal, they might (as I did) overlook that it is the experience of writing that often has greater potential to move the writer to a place of greater understanding of herself and the world rather than the information contained on the page.

With an emphasis on skills-based learning and correct text production in the writing classroom, teachers and students are missing out on the pedagogical benefits of Yagelski's ontological argument. He emphasizes a pedagogy that focuses on the "writer writing" rather than the "writer's writing":

> The text does not disappear in this pedagogy, but rather than being the focus of writing instruction, it becomes a component of the process of inquiry into self and world that the act of writing can be. In this way, the text becomes part of a larger act of inquiry through writing, which in turn becomes a vehicle for truth-seeking . . . In other words, we write as a way of being together in the world—as a way to understand ourselves and our connection to what is around us; in this formulation, we write *with* the text rather than to produce a text.
>
> (8)

As students revise or work on drafts of any writing, Yagelski suggests a pedagogy that asks about the experience that was the focus of writing (not the text). Teaching writing is engaging in writing as an act of inquiry into our own experiences of the world much like Rosenblatt's theory of transactional reading. Writing is participating in the world and who we are in this world. If students can experience and understand writing as such, then when they read, they will be aligned ontologically with the other writer and ready to bear witness. In other words, they will sense a connectedness in being.

The challenge to the English classroom is to cultivate pedagogies that take into account the complexities of human learning and human life that are part of distinct and overlapping global communities (Yagelski). The narrow curriculum that is prescriptive and measurable is an attempt to control such complexity. Yagelski wonders what the world would look like today if we would have always taught kids writing as a way of being. Might it have "opened up a capacity of writing to understand anew their experience of themselves in the world . . . [and] what might the communities they created look like?" (163). In my view, Yagelski is suggesting that writing as a way of being may just contribute to our students' capacity to imagine how our communities *ought* to be, how we *ought* to relate to one another.

Writing as Witnessing

I had written with and for students in the past using Atwell or Murray's writing workshop approach, but I had not developed trust in the process. Perhaps it was pressure to teach skills or difficulty balancing the teaching of reading and writing; nevertheless, every year, despite my best intentions, I would inevitably do more explicit instruction and cut back on in-class writing time. Yagelski's book alerted me to the need to revise my teaching practices. The day after my graduate class met to discuss Yagelski's book, I watched closely as my eighth graders in classroom H103 drafted personal narratives. Some were writing; some were thinking; and, of course, quite a few were fidgeting. I wondered about the sort of community I had created: *How many were witnessing a scene of their lives for the first time? How many were producing a product? And when students would inevitably peer conference their memories, how many would listen to their peer as though it were a privilege to bear witness to that life? Had I taught them to do that?* No. No, I had not. I was not, however, entirely sure how to teach "writing as a way of being."

It was during a professional development day not long after reading Yagelski's work that I first met scholar and teacher-educator Jennifer Berne. In a demonstration lesson, she stood in front of a room full of English teachers and talked through her writing process: an A-to-Z brainstorm activity, a select-and-reject activity to choose her topic, and a graphic organizer to plan her piece. She also made visible and audible her thinking, from anxiety about seeing a blank page to struggling to find the right word. It was a five-minute frenzy, but it was enough for me to see how I might shift the focus of a writing workshop mini-lesson from producing a text to the experience of writing. If I could come to the writing event open to the possibility of experience, I might be able to support the *act* of writing as witnessing rather than writing as a product. I knew that we would write about our lives, and I knew that I would have to *be* and subsequently have to *teach* being vulnerable if we were to draw out what it means to write with and for others.

Over the course of a few weeks, I made time in class for students to witness my writing process. I asked them to simply notice what they noticed, and then we talked about my process and how it felt for them to witness my inner thoughts. Then we'd write together, and I'd ask them to be conscious of their process and the energy in the room. This was my way of trying to tune into the act of writing for our writing community. I made the decision not to have a skill or standard in mind nor any plan for what I would write about other than a personal occurrence that I wanted to explore through writing. I did my best to go to that place and time and make visible my struggle to gather the fragments into some coherent rendering. Here is a sketch of how I try to make visible my writing experience for students with Berne's protocol:

I turn on the overhead projector and document camera. I lay out my notebook, opened to a fresh page. I grab my felt-tip pen and announce that I am going to be Sarah (the person, not the teacher) for a few minutes.

"Just watch me write and listen to me think about my writing, and then we will talk about what you notice."

I do not plan what I am going to write, but I know I want students to think about how something unexpected can spark a memory or move us to action. I have in mind the next text we are going to read (*First They Killed My Father*), so I am hoping to help them write about a childhood memory.

"So I hate a blank page. It stresses me out, almost paralyzes me. I am going to just do some brainstorming to see if I can find a place to start, a place I want to know more about, or a place I want to think about."

I admit that I am drawing a blank and am feeling anxious, so I turn to the back of my notebook, where I have taped a list of writing prompts to spark memories and experiences. I am not opposed to writing prompts if the writer finds them useful. I scan through and then write a few on my blank page: my first funeral (which was when I was ten and my twelve-year-old cousin had just died of leukemia); a special place in my childhood (which was the closet); when my life changed forever (which was when my father moved in with me and my husband). I write the topics, and then I write "so what" next to each, deciding which is worth writing or which "so what" I was most interested in discovering (Atwell).

At this point, students, who are supposed to be *just* noticing, call out to me which topic they want me to write about. Most students are fascinated by the lives of their teachers. I decided on writing about my funeral memory. I talk about (as I write) all the memory bits I can pull together. I was about ten when my cousin, Ray, died. I think he was about twelve, the same age as my older sister, Libby. Ray died of leukemia. I have a vivid memory of where and how my dad told me that Ray died. I have another vivid memory of the car ride to the funeral. I was riding in the "back-back" of the family "sport-about" station wagon; it was raining, and headlights from the cars behind us reflected in the raindrops that fell on the rear windshield just inches from my nose. I talked about how "what happened" was blurry, and why it mattered to my life now was unclear. Then I stopped. It was time to hear what the students noticed (e.g., I got stuck; I brainstormed; I considered the "so what"; I drafted; I talked to myself). And then it was time for them to bear witness to their own childhood.

During the days that followed, we worked through the standard writing process (brainstorming, planning, drafting, conferencing, and revising) in the same way and with different memories. One student wrote about her visit to Poland for a family wedding, playing disco polo and eating *kielbasa*. Another student wrote about her first funeral, too, and then her memory of visiting her father in jail. Side by side we wrote our memories. We'd cross out and erase words on the page; we'd turn to a neighbor and talk through some part that we just couldn't capture with words. As I talked through my own writing, I was careful to deliberate the choices, always asking if it was the truth and how the story was, in fact, my own. I shared my frustration with my feeling that the words ending up on the page were far from a "totalizable account" of my experience (2).

I tried out different techniques to try to call forth a memory or fill in gaps. For example, I tried writing my memory first from the voice of a young Sarah and then as my older self to see how the narrator represented my memory differently. I wondered out loud which rendering would be more authentic, even fair. In a few writing events, I had to admit that I was filling in gaps with a bit of fiction or even with what I felt happened but could not recall for certain. For those scenes, I tried a different typeface or asterisks to alert my reader that I was being more inventive. I suggested this was an ethical obligation I had to my reader. And dialogue, while wholly inventive for my piece, helped me imagine (even project) how my father might have comforted me, for example. It was a childhood memory after all. I could ask my siblings, but I could no longer ask my father about the memory because he has passed; even so, whatever my family remembers from my cousin's death would also be a memory and, thus, partial and subjective. I wondered aloud if we should even tell our stories, suggesting it was a little unethical because of the problem of truth. How can I really know "what happened"? I tried to model, to make visible, my "double attentiveness" (Simon and Eppert). How did I know what happened? What were the limits to what I *could* know and tell with any kind of authority? And what was my ethical responsibility to the reader-listener? How can I help her experience this memory alongside me in an authentic way?

I even wondered if I was being too personal as a teacher. My greatest concern was whether I was teaching students to bear witness to one another's lives or whether I was teaching them to be spectators, even voyeurs. Some students were excited to hear my memory of people sobbing or of what my young cousin looked like in his casket. For the most part, however, I felt like students were bearing witness to my life as I was witnessing my childhood memory for the first time. When I looked up from my paper, some students made eye contact with me as if to say, *Go on, I'm with you.* Others looked down, perhaps uncomfortable with the level of intimacy (i.e., hearing a teacher share personal things), perhaps just showing respect for my memory. As a child, I did not have the capacity to be aware or to comprehend the event of my cousin's death; I did not have the capacity to fully comprehend how that memory shaped my understanding of death. The students listening to me so attentively during my writing—and listening to one another during conferences—illuminated our human desire to know about one another's lives. I am not sure that I was able to make explicit in any way how subjective and even rhetorical my writing was, but I think the students understood (as I do now) the vital role we each play as listeners in one another's lives, for without a listener, our testimony would not exist.

It has been my privilege all these years as a teacher to listen to students' stories about their lives. I have read thousands of personal narratives, but in making visible the act of writing alongside my students, I experienced what it means to witness my own life through writing, to enter a relationship with language, to depend on language to help me establish an account of my experience, and to trust my students to be my witness.

During writing workshop, I observed powerful moments as small groups of students read their stories to one another with respect and compassion. Indeed, peer response is an act of community building and shared meaning making, as Yagelski argues, because it is not limited to improving texts. I think that while I had essentially taught the writing standards by going through the writing process with students and doing mini-lessons on some writing techniques, my "objective" was to illuminate and be conscious of the activity of writing. The products were secondary and perhaps better because they were not our focus. I think we made a lot of progress toward using writing as a way of witnessing our own lives and as a way of teaching us to bear witness to one another's lives.

From Writing to Reading

I wondered what would happen if we took this way of thinking about writing and listening to literature. Could we bring this understanding of the experience of writing, of narrative construction, of the rhetorical moves the writer makes to express and communicate to the reading experience of books? Would the students read a memoir, produced outside the writing workshop, with greater understanding of the writer's experience? Would this be another valued story and writer in our community of writers and listeners, or would this text be an outsider and thus an object of feeling and sight?

Loung Ung, in her talk "Writing the Truth," explained what moment prompted her to write her memoir *First They Killed My Father*. Born in 1970 in Phnom Penh, Loung Ung is a survivor of the killing fields of Cambodia. Pol Pot and the Khmer Rouge regime systematically killed nearly 1.7 million Cambodians, including Ung's parents, two of her siblings, and twenty other relatives. Only a child at the time, Ung was forced to train and perform duties of a child soldier in order to survive. In the three-minute clip of the talk, Ung tells us the "four little words" that prompted her to write her 2000 memoir: Pol Pot is dead. She says that when she heard these words on the radio, "My heart shattered like a stained glass dropped on a concrete floor. My eyes in such shock that I could not blink . . . I could only hate." Pol Pot was characterized in the report as "kind" and "gentlemanly" and "charismatic." While she wanted to "crush" the radio, instead she said, "I could . . . pick up my pen and tell my story and tell the truth about the mass murderer that he was."

In the weeks that followed the transition from writing workshop to reading workshop, students considered more deeply truth telling and bearing witness. Ung's memoir helped us understand storytelling in a more public context, what it would mean to publish our personal narratives for the world to read and witness. First, we have someone, a survivor, who willingly relives or perhaps really witnesses for the first time in the act of storytelling an experience, and second, we have the other who is that survivor's companion in experiencing the story (the reader-witness). In other words, the reader is a secondary witness, also bearing witness to the events, trauma, and atrocity, seeking an understanding of that which is unimaginable and, perhaps, unknowable, but no less impactful as a way of being in the world. To help us understand this somewhat existential experience, my class read a blog post called "Talking Wounds" that summarizes several points that I first read (and discussed earlier) in Shoshana Felman and Dori Laub's *Testimony: Crises of Witnessing in Literature, Psychoanalysis and History*. This blog, written by visual artist Marilene Oliver and human rights philosopher Sophie Oliver, "seeks to explore ways of ethically discussing and representing human rights atrocities." Oliver and Oliver quote French philosopher Jean-François Lyotard, who describes the model of listener as one "who actively and ethically listens, recognising the voice and subjectivity of the testifier in the process is not merely an additional benefit; (s)he is a vital element without which the testimony would not exist" (qtd. in "Talking Wounds"). The blog, Ung's memoir, and our own writing experiences transacted to help us make sense of our responsibility as writers and readers of testimony and other agents of memory; we are vital elements.

At this point, I need to pause to admit that I initially read *First They Killed My Father* in 2006 because of the Illinois Genocide Education Mandate requiring me to teach about the Cambodian genocide. Prior to 2012, however, I had not read this book whole-class, though Lincoln had a class set in its book room. Instead, I had jigsawed the genocides listed in the mandate as a way of covering the genocides (Chapter 2). Jigsaw is a technique whereby the teacher arranges students into home groups; each group member is assigned a different text to read on their own or with members from other groups assigned the same text; then members return to their home group to "piece together" the information (similarities, differences) gleaned from each text. In other words, only a handful of students each year had read Ung's account of the genocidal processes that killed her family, and they were responsible for retelling Ung's story for their peers. Clearly, there are ethical issues with my past practice that I have tried to illuminate here and in previous chapters. The dilemmas I faced as an English teacher trying to meet a state mandate about human rights violations were so profound that

I pursued a doctorate in English so that I could research these dilemmas for myself and others.

My experiences learning and teaching about genocide, a simultaneous process, prompted a shift in my treatment of *First They Killed My Father* from a book about genocide to an inquiry of public testimony. I found this notion of bearing witness essential to understanding the stories we tell and the stories we hear, essential to developing conscious readers. For Felman and Laub, the listener (or reader) is "party to the creation of knowledge" (15). Teachers following state mandates (whether that means teaching about genocide or the Common Core State Standards) are a vital element without which those mandates would not exist; our task then is do take up this role actively and ethically, which means considering what and how we *ought* to teach.

In 2012, then, we read Ung's memoir as a class. I did not want anyone to be alone in witnessing her life, nor did I want any student to feel responsible for retelling Ung's experiences as a child soldier in Khmer Rouge Cambodia. We read the first chapter of *First They Killed My Father* for narratorial style primarily. I wanted students to notice how the grown-up Ung was witnessing her childhood, translating her experiences through sensory language, imagery, thoughts, feelings and observations, dialogue, poetic language, and perspective:

> Ma says I stomp around like a cow dying of thirst. She's tried many times to teach me the proper way for a young lady to walk. First, you connect your heel to the ground, then roll the ball of your feet on the earth while your toes curl up painfully. Finally you end up with your toes gently pushing you off the ground. All this is supposed to be done gracefully, naturally, and quietly. It all sounds too complicated and painful to me. Besides, I am happy stomping around.
>
> (3)

Students heard the voice of five-year-old Loung, and they noticed how she is representing herself as a precocious, middle-class, tomboy-ish child who can't seem to please her mother but shares a special bond with her father.

Students began a text-based discussion journal to note passages where they became conscious of their witnessing. How are you relating to Ung, whose life seems so distant from yours? What aspects of that passage make it difficult for you to attend to Ung's memory? How is Ung using language to help her establish an account of experience? What words and phrases resonate with you? What images help or disturb? Are those necessary for Ung? For her readers? After reading, students converted their notes into interpretive questions for their peers, and we held a fishbowl seminar. For that class, a fishbowl seminar entailed an inside and outside group. The inside group of four to ten students sat in a circle with their notes to discuss selected passages for the purpose of deepening their experience and understanding of the text. The outside group practiced witnessing the discussion by making notes on communication dynamics and the discussion topics. For our first fishbowl, it did not take long for students to express sympathy for the child narrator and how she was "unreliable." The innocent voice, so young, couldn't possibly remember this detail, they offered. Can we trust her? Is it a matter of trust or in recognizing how this narrator was Ung's link to events? How can testimony be considered nonfiction? (Students did not immediately make the connection to our writing workshop.)

We read some public critiques of Ung's memoir because I wanted students to know that they were cueing into real issues with writing and reading testimony for the public. I wanted them to see how for other survivors who have memories of Cambodia's killing fields, Ung's writing has very real implications. Contributors to a website moderated by the Cambodian cultural group named the Khmer Institute write this critique (among others):

> To further impress her readers, Ung actually goes so far as to claim to have shot an AK-47 (142). To be only seven years old and malnourished and still capable of firing an AK-47, a weapon that is even difficult for a full grown adult inexperienced in its use to manage, Ung had to have had superhuman strength. The Khmer Rouge were extremists, but it is hardly believable that they would give such an important and valuable piece of weaponry to a little girl at a time when they were killing people with axes and machetes in order to save bullets. Finally, keeping in mind Ung's constant refrain about how the Khmer Rouge did not trust and hated light-skinned people, why would they then give such a weapon to a light-skinned girl? She explains, "They think I am one of them, one of the pure base children"; but how could they if she is so different in appearance that, as the reader is often reminded, she is constantly discriminated against?
>
> (Hor, Lay, and Quinn)

Students were in an uproar. Was Ung trying to "impress her readers"? Maybe. Hadn't we all tried to impress our readers to some degree with our stories? But doesn't desperation make us capable of "superhuman strength" at times? And hadn't Ung's light skin been camouflaged by dirt or by her work ethic? And remember, the students would argue, Ung was a child. We had to trust that the adult Ung was doing the best she could to remember.

Students, working from their personal, emotional responses, seemed to be attending to Simon and Eppert's "double attentiveness." They were getting at epistemological questions and exploring the rhetoricality of that text when they were questioning Ung's choice to write her memoir from the voice of her child self. They noticed Ung's choice to italicize, indicating sections that were more inventive. Ung's typography worked to establish trust with the reader because the shift in typeface told her listeners that she had reached the limits of her memory but that she was using writing as a way of investigating what lies beyond. The ethical practice of witnessing (as a reader) means being conscious of how the person (in this case, Ung) is translating her experiences across time and space, and the students were engaged in this project. To be clear, the "ethical" part of reading as witnessing is not about sympathy per se; it is building a capacity in readers to recognize the process that made public that which was once silent.

Conclusion

When the state writes a text that mandates a unit of instruction about the Holocaust to "study the events of the Nazi atrocities of 1933 to 1945," how do we, teacher-readers, read such a text ("Illinois Genocide Curriculum Mandate")? And when the state revises that text to recognize "that crimes of genocide continue to be perpetrated across the globe . . . and to deter indifference to crimes against humanity and human suffering wherever they may occur," how do we read that text? What do these texts attempt to represent? I admitted earlier that what inspired me to select, order, and share *First They Killed My Father* was such a text: a curriculum mandate crafted by elected members of the state of Illinois. I think it is worth considering how this text moved me as a reader and writer, ultimately informing my practice as a teacher and path as a human being. I assumed a certain contract with the writers (Illinois legislators), almost a moral relationship, and felt compelled to attend to the call to action. At first, as Hesford argues, the focus was on how I and students would react to the human rights violations, but we learned how to be more conscious of how we were viewing the "spectacle" and shifted our focus and responsibility to the people who needed us to bear witness and remember.

My pedagogical choice to read *First They Killed My Father* with eighth graders not as a vessel of information but as a testimony to which students would bear witness was a deliberate effort to nurture students' consciousness of how they are ethically implicated by the texts they write and read. They are not spectators but rather witnesses who can either distance themselves from the human beings represented or attend to them and in doing so bear witness to a life mediated by language, in this case, that of Loung Ung. Of course, as I have been arguing, teachers have a responsibility to nurture and support ethical witnessing. In our writing workshop, I had tried to illuminate writing as witnessing and the relationship among writing, reading, and bearing witness. I think by shifting the focus of our work to the activity of writing, we created a community interested in writing as a process of testifying and truth seeking rather than writing as a product, thus calling attention to how events and experiences are always mediated.

While I recognized the writing experience as a way of witnessing my life and seeking truth, while I tried to support this way of being in the classroom, and while I think it prepared us to then bear witness to Loung Ung's testimony in *First They Killed My Father*, I think that some students did not see the text as an alignment between themselves (reader-listener-witness) and

Ung (testifier-witness). From what I saw in faces as we read and heard in seminar discussions, Ung's narrative did not stir in them a shift from spectator to witness. Perhaps I failed to engage students in this transaction, or perhaps the "hazards" of listening were too much for some students. Reading as witnessing is complex and hazardous. There is much uncertainty in the transactional spaces among students, teachers, texts, and beyond. Ignoring this transactional space is, indeed, easier than attending to its uncertainty. Nevertheless, I think we have a responsibility to teach the ethical practice of witnessing, for it will prepare our students to go out into the world understanding that there are agents of memory out there (people, social media, TV, movies, books) addressing our students, positioning them to be global witnesses to historical events and human suffering. What will they do? How will they relate to the distant sufferer? Will they turn away? Will they act complicitously (Rentschler)? Will their interpretations perpetuate hierarchies and stereotypes? Or will they take up their epistemological and ethical responsibilities as readers and human beings?

My hope is that students will know that when they read testimony they recognize that while they are not getting the whole story, the fragments and gaps are valuable and necessary. Their responsibility to the testimony (and to the story) is epistemological (i.e., how is it possible that this writer knows what happened, what are the limits to what the writer can say, what lies beyond those limits) and ethical, as in accepting the obligation to attend to the human being who testifies. Ultimately, our students are not only addressed by the world agents of memory, but they are agents of memory who will use language to mediate events and experience of their lives. What practical and moral claims will they put upon their listeners? Will they know and practice their ethical responsibility to their subject and their audience? Our ethical responsibility as teachers, then, is to cultivate in our students habits of mind that will impact not only their learning in classrooms, not only their choices in colleges and careers, but ultimately the roles they take up in society.

Works Cited

Atwell, Nancie. *In the Middle.* Portsmouth, NH: Boynton/Cook, 1987. Print.

Berne, Jennifer. *The Writing-Rich High School Classroom: Engaging Students in the Writing Workshop.* New York: Guildford Press, 2008. Print.

Calkins, Lucy. *The Art of Teaching Writing.* Portsmouth, NH: Heinemann Educational Books, 1994. Print.

Dutro, Elizabeth, and Monette McIver. "Imagining a Writer's Life: Extending the Connection Between Readers and Books." Ed. Shelby Wolf, Karen Coats, Patricia A. Enciso, and Christine Jenkins. *Handbook of Research on Children's and Young Adult Literature.* New York: Routledge, 2010. 92–107. Print.

Felman, Shoshana, and Dori Laub. *Testimony: Crises of Witnessing in Literature, Psychoanalysis, and History.* New York: Routledge, 1991. Print.

Graves, Donald. *Writing: Teachers and Children at Work.* Portsmouth, NH: Heinemann, 1983. Print.

Hor, Soneath, Sody Lay, and Grantham Quinn. "First They Killed My Father: A Definitive Analysis." *Khmer Institute.* Web.

"Illinois Genocide Curriculum Mandate." *Genocide Education Network of Illinois*.org. 2011. Web.

Murray, Donald. *A Writer Teaches Writing.* Boston: Houghton Mifflin Company, 1985. Print.

Oliver, Sophie, and Marilene Oliver. "Bearing Witness to the Witness: Some Thoughts on Hearing Wounds Talk." *Talking Wounds.* 12 May. 2011. Web.

Rosenblatt, Louise. *Literature as Exploration.* New York: Appleton Century, 1938. 4th ed. New York: Modern Language Association, 1983. Print.

Simon, Roger, and Claudia Eppert. "Pedagogy and the Witnessing Testimony of Historical Trauma." *Canadian Journal of Education.* 22.2 (1997): 175–191. Web.

Totten, Samuel. *Teaching About Genocide: Issues, Approaches, and Resources.* Greenwich, CT: Information Age Publishing, 2004. Print.

Ung, Loung. *First They Killed My Father: A Daughter of Cambodia Remembers.* New York: Harper Collins, 2000. Print.

———. "Loung Ung: Authors of Our Lives." *Omega.org.* 18 Apr. 2012. Web.

Yagelski, Robert P. *Writing as a Way of Being: Writing Instruction, Nonduality, and the Crisis of Sustainability.* New York: Hampton Press, 2011. Print.

A Teacher's Testimony

Michael Krzysztofiak is a high school English and history teacher in Chicago public schools. Here he reflects on his experience reading *First They Killed My Father* with his students:

> Teaching about genocide is not easy (this might be the understatement of the century). The topic is emotionally charged and before teaching it, one must determine how much, or how little, to censor. I believe that the best approach is one in which kids are not shielded from the horrors and atrocities that have scarred humanity. Protecting students from the historical record does not erase what has happened; rather, censoring the past (or present, in the case of Syria and Burundi) can actually stop kids from experiencing a transformational educational experience. I know that as teachers we have to walk a fine line of what is acceptable. We are beholden to administrator and parent expectations, standards-based teaching, and the constant barrage of state and district testing. But the Common Core and standardized tests do not measure two of the most important attributes students should be taught in school: empathy and a sense of social justice. Exposing students to genocide allows them to examine and analyze the dark side

of humanity, and the sense of hope that springs from the resilience of survivors.

I believe that as teachers we need to trust our students to be able to handle a complex topic like genocide. Furthermore, I think that students need to be empowered to wrestle with the issues without a strictly prescribed definition of what they need to "get" from the lesson/unit. Students need to find their own voice and express the emotions and ideas that come naturally from this voice. That is not to say that students should be thrown into the deep end without any support; rather, students should be helped along their journey by the teacher as the facilitator of ideas. With that in mind, I tried to create an assignment that would allow students to explore their own reactions to genocide and atrocities as expressed in their own words. Along the way, students showed me a deep sense of empathy and social agency that transformed me as a teacher.

Students need to know that their voices are important and should be heard. To that end, I capped my genocide unit with a letter-writing campaign to President Obama. We had read *First They Killed My Father*, and studied the Bosnian and Rwandan Genocides before our capstone project. The students were dismayed that even after all of the promises that the world had made after the Holocaust, genocide had never been eradicated. After some students asked me about the Syrian refugee crisis, I decided to let them explore the horrors of this conflict. I let them read and reflect on survivor stories, and allowed them to research the auto-genocide committed by the Assad regime. What I found was that the vast majority of students were visibly shaken by the stories and images that they were exposed to, and they expressed a desire to try to do something about it. With the Syrian refugee crisis raging, I gave the students a very basic outline, and asked them to write letters to President Obama to discuss our policy towards the refugees. I didn't force the kids to do the assignment, as I knew that I needed to respect differing viewpoints. However, the vast majority of students wrote passionate letters that showed how much they had learned from exploring the darkness of genocide. There was no specific structure, or word count, but what they produced made me the proudest I have ever been as a teacher. Students wrote with a passion and conviction that no five-paragraph essay could ever match. I didn't censor kids when they started with lines like, "how many more three year olds have to wash up dead on the shores of Turkey before the world starts to pay attention?" I didn't chastise them for challenging our president to uphold the American values that we preach. When kids are given a chance to explore difficult subjects through their own lens, the results can be truly transformative.

There is this persistent stereotype that teenagers don't care about anything outside of their own world, and I think that nothing is further from the truth. My students have proven this to me through their compassion, empathy, and sense of social justice. As of me writing this, we have not received anything back from the White House, but either way, my students know that they have made a difference by making their voices heard!

10 Whole-Class Reading, Research, and Activism

By reading genocide literature alongside students, teachers can foster in students not just awareness for the plight of other people (i.e., knowledge of or about) but a habitual inclination to analyze and become conscious of how we are conditioned to respond to human rights violations and scenes of atrocities by texts and images and then, perhaps, intervene.

In this chapter, I provide a limited overview of the Guatemalan genocide before taking you into my classroom story of how we read Ben Mikaelsen's *Tree Girl*. I illuminate how we worked together to uncover the ethical, emotional, and rational appeals of the text, which prompted a multigenre inquiry project, a presentation at a city youth summit, and a community fundraising campaign.

Genocide in Guatemala

In the early 1980s, the Guatemalan army instituted Operation Sophia, a military program aimed at stopping guerrillas by destroying the civilian bases in which they hid. The scorched-earth policy of special units known as Kaibiles destroyed 626 villages and massacred more than 200,000 Mayans; the U.S. government supported and trained these death squads at the School of the Americas, providing weapons and helicopters in the name of anti-Communist policies. Many of the victims were buried in mass graves in the Guatemalan Highlands.

The exhumation of mass graves by the Guatemalan Forensic Anthropology Foundation, a nonprofit, nongovernmental organization, began in 1990 and by 2004 had investigated more than three hundred burial sites and recovered nearly three thousand human remains. The foundation and current director Fredy Peccerelli are responding to various groups of survivors who, in 1990, began reporting the clandestine graves, which contain the bodies of Maya massacred during the government's 1980 "scorched-earth" policy. It was only in 1994 that the Historical Clarification Commission, Guatemala's truth commission, was established by the Oslo Accords. The Accords attempted to end Guatemala's civil war, a war in which an estimated 200,000 Maya were massacred. The Commission concluded:

> [T]he structure and nature of economic, cultural and social relations in Guatemala are marked by profound exclusion, antagonism and

> conflict—a reflection of its colonial history. The proclamation of independence in 1821, an event prompted by the country's elite, saw the creation of an authoritarian State which excluded the majority of the population. It was racist in its precepts and practices, and served to protect the economic interests of the privileged minority. The evidence for this, throughout Guatemala's history, but particularly so during the armed confrontation, lies in the fact that the violence was fundamentally directed by the State against the excluded, the poor and above all, the Mayan people, as well as against those who fought for justice and greater social equality.

There is a pan-Maya Movement to revive Mayan languages and culture happening in Guatemala in response to the years of compulsory linguistic assimilation, religious conversion, and military service that began with the Spanish colonization and continued with the modern Guatemalan state's efforts to eradicate cultural difference. The survivors' groups appropriated the symbol of "genocide" to resist further oppression by advocating for the exhumation of the bodies and for criminal proceedings to hold members of the Guatemalan military responsible for what the Commission determined was, in fact, genocide; however, the other aim is to revive indigenous cultures and languages. Is the pan-Maya movement nationalistic? Under these "other conditions" does the word "genocide" have a different meaning (Bakhtin 428)?

The rhetoric of "genocide" and rhetoric of nationalism are similar in that both are deceptive. For example, the guerrillas in Guatemala, made up of predominantly middle-class students, activists, and former government workers, cultivated an image of solidarity with the peasants (Maya and poor ladinos) using the rhetoric of Guatemalan nationalism: "We fight for a free Guatemala where Indian and non-Indians are equal" (French). While there were some peasants who took up arms with the guerrillas, most were stuck in the middle of the conflict between the government and the guerrillas, wanting only to work their *milpas*, agricultural land, and live the lives of their ancestors.

A central component in the pan-Maya movement, however, is the dialectic of language ideology. According to Brigittine M. French, author of *Maya Ethnolinguistic Identity: Violence, Cultural Rights, and Modernity in Highland Guatemala*, "The Maya movement seeks to create a Guatemalan nation reconstituted and redefined by the politics of cultural difference" (30). The Maya are revitalizing indigenous languages to strategically challenge the homogenizing and exclusionary goals of modernity fundamental to the 1980 genocide. Thus, the diverse Mayan languages link to create an ideal of a collective in a nationalist sense. In this movement, there are convictions of difference for the purpose of legitimizing autonomy. The problematic of the movement, however, is that to produce new indigenous experts to regiment language and culture requires the construction of an apparatus of social engineering, some iteration of a school, with directors, teachers, curriculum, and students. In 2003, the Guatemalan government passed *La Ley de Idiomas Nacionales* to promote languages used by Maya, Garifuna, and Xinca. Thus, in a sense, the discourse of progress for the Maya is a revival of state structures they seek to resist. To put it another way, the indigenous languages will now be taught in schools; people will now be identified by language or, more importantly, categories of culture. Classifying people and assigning symbols to them (i.e., language) may create ethnic pride, but it also creates friction. This situation illustrates the rhetoricality of the word "genocide" because the word has been used to prompt people to engage in a paradoxical initiative—namely, to revive indigenous languages and cultures that are separate from the homogenous state in ways that rely on state apparatuses.

Rhetorical Appeals in *Tree Girl*

Since 2006, eighth graders at Lincoln Junior High have read a young-adult novel, *Tree Girl* by Ben Mikaelsen. Set in the 1980s, *Tree Girl* is the story of Gabriela (Gabi) Flores, an Indio (Mayan) girl living a traditional life in the highlands of Guatemala who is spirited and smart. Gabi practices the art of Mayan weaving, walks hours to sell corn and coffee at the market, and is the only girl in her cantón to attend school, where she learns Spanish, a *lingua franca* among more than twenty Mayan languages. At the beginning of the novel, Gabi is preparing for her *quinceañera*, her fifteenth birthday, when guerrilla warfare comes to her area. Government soldiers are fighting "Communist" guerrillas and driving the Indios from their land. Mikaelsen's writing is rich with imagery of a world so respected by Mayans: trees that bring Gabi "closer to heaven" winds that "carry the voices of her ancestors," and "small rivers of tears" that she wipes away with her *huipil* (a woven blouse). The students take to Gabi immediately with a sense of respect for her character, such as when she traps a group of troublesome boys in a tree, helps her brother kill a pig for her quinceañera, and teachers younger children at school. When soldiers attack her cantón and when Gabi witnesses a pueblo being burned from the safety of a tree, students are moved and troubled by her vow to never climb another tree. They express sympathy for Gabi's distress and read on to discover how she will cope with what she has witnessed.

In later chapters of *Tree Girl*, when it becomes clear to the students that the Mayans are being targeted by the Guatemalan government, a few notice the social forces at work—the classification of Indios and Latinos, the language of dehumanization, the policies to manage and control movement of Mayans, and the systematic mass violence. Eighth graders, those who learned about genocide in seventh grade, recognize that Gabi's troubles are just beginning. They anticipate the violence to come, and they revise their understanding of genocide as they compare what they learned and experienced in *Hotel Rwanda* to what they are learning and experiencing in *Tree Girl*. Indeed, students shift between efferent and aesthetic reading stances. Students without prior knowledge or reading experiences about genocide relate Gabi's Guatemalan traditions to their own Mexican traditions or appreciate Mikaelsen's use of similes or connect the loss of a parent to the death of Gabi's mother. All of these reader responses are important to finding meaning in *Tree Girl*.

One October morning in 2012, with books and notebooks in hand, we turned to Chapter 9 of *Tree Girl*: Just after Gabi's cantón in the highlands of Guatemala had been burned by government forces, Gabi and her younger sister Alicia are making the two hundred–mile trek towards Mexico's refugee camps when they come upon a mother in labor. Gabi helps birth the child, but the mother does not survive, and so in order to find food for the baby, Gabi hides her sister and the baby under a bush and goes to a nearby market, a pueblo apparently untouched by the scorched-earth policy of the Guatemalan army. There, she meets Mother Lopez, a nun who intended to help Gabi until the soldiers surrounded the market. Gabi runs to safety in the branches of a *machichi* tree, and from above the pueblo, she and we bear witness to the soldiers' systematic massacre of every living being in the pueblo over a two-day period. Here is an excerpt:

> The pile of burning bodies made a small hill in the plaza, and a wretched scorched smell filled the air. Those devils would have kept killing if there had been a thousand people, but by late afternoon every living human and creature had been murdered except me . . . The men went to the *pilas*, the big washing sinks near the church where women washed their clothes. They shaved their faces and took turns washing the blood from their uniforms and skin so that they could return home to their own wives and children. I know that their souls could not be so easily cleaned. After what had happened, I hoped they were all damned to hell . . . Climbing that tree had not been an act of bravery. It was the act of a desperate coward. Everyone else had faced the soldiers except me. I had hidden while others died. By being the Tree Girl, I had been a coward.
>
> (*Tree Girl* 136–138)

Chapter 9 is arguably the most graphic chapter of the novel. Before reading this novel, I sent home a letter explaining my rationale for the novel, inviting parents to read the novel, and offering the opportunity for parents to opt out their child from reading certain chapters. I prefer to be alongside my students reading graphic scenes so that we can experience the text and consider its implications together, but I respect that some students have traumatic pasts that genocidal scenes can trigger. And so in some cases, I conference with students privately about the passages, and we talk about how the author is representing these unimaginable scenes. For the most part, however, students read and are satisfied by the graphic representations of genocide. In fact, one student that morning said, "I love genocide."

I have heard it before. My gut coils in the moments before I respond; I know this response offers an opportunity to explore how genocide is represented and why. The student's life experiences, the author's life experiences, the novel's subject, the words on the page, my life experiences, the classroom—all these elements are transacting in those moments. Having read *Tree Girl* with hundreds of students, I still experience a pedagogical crisis; I am concerned and even uncertain about the value of violence in young-adult literature, but this discomfort pushes me to do the inquiry with the students. This is why "ethical sympathy" is an essential pedagogical force in reading literature. I wondered (and still wonder) if it is ethical for writers to depict graphic scenes in texts intended for young-adult readers. I wonder why student-readers *want* to read graphic scenes. Moreover, I wonder if it is ethical for me, as an agent of memory, to select a text like *Tree Girl* to remember the Guatemalan genocide.

Space for Feeling

Sympathy is important because it involves an emotional connection—a feeling *for*—another person (including the person depicted in the text). Ethical sympathy is important because, as teachers, we want students to develop the urge to alleviate the suffering of others, to feel compelled to think about and imagine how we *ought* to relate to others and what ought to be done to prevent further suffering. Beyond these two separate terms, this phrase is important for English teachers because ethical sympathy is a concept we can talk about as readers, which has the potential to foster thoughtful social action or ways of reacting to graphic images and events beyond the classroom. Students' aesthetic responses to texts begin long before they come to the text; there is a history to their lives for which we, as teachers, cannot wholly account, which students bring to our classrooms and to that which they read. While some students respond to a traumatic scene with deep sympathy, others are excited by it, and still others turn away—distancing themselves from the distress or denying themselves a tear. This is an essential feature of a reading event that schema-oriented methods undervalue.

The reader's aesthetic response to literature is vital in making and revising meaning. Rosenblatt defines aesthetic response as such:

> [A] free, uninhibited emotional reaction to a work of art or literature as an absolutely *necessary* condition of sound literary judgment. However, it is not, to use the logician's term, a *sufficient* condition. Without a real impact between the book and the mind of the reader, there can be no process of judgment at all, but honest recognition of one's own reaction is not in itself sufficient to ensure sound critical opinion.
>
> (72, emphasis original)

Transactional reading calls for an instructional approach that encourages readers to experience the work aesthetically, noting *how* it appeals to them as unique readers and thinkers. To be clear, the purpose for reading is not to arrive at the right interpretation of the text (e.g., New Criticism); the text is not a static artifact that means the same to every reader; the reader is not dependent on the teacher to build background knowledge or provide reading activities to guide comprehension before they even read the text (e.g., schema theory). We want students to make some judgment about what they read. The reason we read something for ourselves (rather than relying on someone to tell us what the text is about) is because the aesthetic experience is irreducible. Our ability to understand and act upon the world is dependent upon our aesthetic experience because it helps us recognize our agency as irreducible to a number, a rating, or a score. To hide or deny discussions of readers' aesthetic responses and how those inform meaning is, in my view, unethical, because it hides or denies our humanity.

To be clear, comprehending the text is important, but it is not sufficient in understanding the text. Authors deliberately appeal to a reader's emotions just as they appeal to logic. By ignoring the text as a personal experience for the reader, readers miss out on the rhetorical nature of the text and their responsibility as readers to make a judgment about what they read.

Aesthetic responses, once invited into the classroom, invite a more substantial and thorough inquiry and critique of the text. Creators of the new Common Core State Standards would have teachers minimizing emotions and feelings when reading, but feelings compel action.

We can look to Holocaust literature scholars to help us understand how our students are responding to genocide literature, why they are responding as they do, and for ideas how to support students in developing a capacity for conscious reading that can draw from and accommodate these emotional responses. Gary Weissman's *Fantasies of Witnessing: Postwar Efforts to Experience the Holocaust* suggests that some people who study genocide, specifically the Holocaust, have a desire "to feel closer to that horror" (5, 209). Weissman makes clear that all attempts to understand the Holocaust are insufficient; all the films and books and poems can only hope to convey some experience of it, but these, too, are inadequate. Thus, perhaps readers just want to get as close as they can, and for that, they let their hearts race a bit more, open their eyes wider, and respond with heightened emotions.

Another perspective is that students experience the text as a bridge connecting them to the past. Alison Landsberg, in *Prosthetic Memory: The Transformation of American Remembrance in the Age of Mass Culture*, suggests that readers have benefitted from increased access to film, social media, and Internet media, which has made it possible to learn from pasts that are not theirs. Students bring this experience to their reading. Texts then, work as a prosthesis between an individual and a historical narrative about the past that actually creates an experience and makes it possible for an individual to have a "deep felt memory" of the past that she did not live. From this perspective, readers are making new memories when they read.

But what about the "I love genocide" response or the desire to read and reread graphic passages that we notice in our teen readers? Kaplan, in *Unwanted Beauty: Aesthetic Pleasure in Holocaust Representation*, argues aesthetic pleasure deepens the search for understanding; "pleasure" is a catalyst for understanding in part because it makes the reader wonder, as I did earlier, if there is something indecent or unethical about this beauty (47). Wendy Hesford, in *Spectacular Rhetorics*, suggests that our students, as Western readers, have developed a habituated response to stories about trauma. Because the exploited or violated person in most literature read in schools is most often depicted as foreign, that is, racially or ethnically different and non-autonomous, and because typically there is a Western figure who saves the foreign victim, readers project *their* lives as that which the victim should hope for, which makes the reader feel pity, even guilt (175).

What Hesford describes is a phenomenon that I have occasionally seen in my own classroom. It is not uncommon for me to hear my compassionate students want to bring trauma victims to America for a better life or to, because of this aesthetic pleasure, feel more grateful for their lives. One former student, Gabriela, said in response to the Guatemalan genocide,

> all these people were dying . . . and here I am in school and I can learn while someone else can't . . . [School's] hard for me but I can't give up. It's like I'm doing the work for that person. They can't do it, so I'll do it for them.

Imagine discussing these scholarly texts alongside literature with our students and engaging in discussions about how the texts are accessing our pasts and eliciting our sympathies. I had these conversations with my eighth graders. No, the texts were not in textbooks published by some corporation. I did not ask students to take multiple-choice tests on aesthetic response. We had discussions—in big groups, in small groups, in individual conferences. They were not easy discussions, and we did not come to any easy answers or even any agreement as to why some of us wanted to reread graphic scenes while others skipped over them and why some of us cried while others were angry. Making space in the English classroom for reader response and this contemporary analysis of reader response as a class can stimulate a desire among our students to understand how texts work to move us to feel, think, and act.

In sum, then, the sympathy-eliciting function of literature has the potential to not only connect us to experiences we have not lived but to truly illuminate habits of mind and increase consciousness of how our experiences transact with the images and texts we read. Misson and Morgan, in *Critical*

Literacy and the Aesthetic: Transforming the English Classroom (2006), capture the potential of the literary experiences well here:

> [Readers] find themselves in sympathy with the worldview being represented in [the text], or they find it enlarges their worldview. Having consented to be managed by the text in this way, readers take delight in all that it has to offer. And so they feel replete as readers who have been enabled to have their desires evoked and satisfied, perhaps in new or intensified ways, and who have been shown a world whose ideas resonate with or extend their ideas of how things are or can be. As they sense the congruence of the form that realises [sic] its world, their ideological alignment matches their aesthetic engagement with the text.
>
> (97)

Space for Community Reading

Up until this point, I've been talking about how attending to emotional response prompts discussion related to how our sympathies are elicited by texts. If we stopped our discussion here, it would be easy to think that aesthetic readings are limited to the interaction between an individual reader and the text. However, students are reading in a classroom; they are part of a community of readers. The benefits from reading in a social context like the English classroom is that a reader can discover how her personal experiences and emotions potentially bias or distort understanding. Extending the reading process beyond "the self" helps readers recognize how prior experiences construct certain reading experiences and interpretations.

English teachers have created literature circles and reading groups for years, often with jobs or role sheets to organize discussions (e.g., discussion director, literary luminary, word watcher, etc.). Sometimes a whole-class discussion can work as a large book group in a Socratic seminar or fishbowl discussion, but why do we read in groups? What is the benefit when it comes to reading literature?

The new Common Core State Standards virtually abandon Rosenblatt's insights by emphasizing close reading: "A significant body of research links the close reading of complex texts—whether the student is a struggling reader or advanced—to significant gains in reading proficiency and finds close reading to be a key component of college and career readiness" (Boyles). Thus, in 2014, Rosenblatt's work with reader response is still excluded in favor of New Criticism's view that content *within* the text is part of the meaning of the text; no appeal to the authority or intention of the author or to the reader's experience is permitted in discussions with New Critics. Of course, there may be a question on the test regarding "author's purpose" on a high-stakes test, but essentially what the English classroom emphasizes is close reading, a systematic and objective method of interpretation that excludes the reader's response, the author's intention, historical and cultural contexts, and moralistic bias from analysis. Textbook companies have already aligned their products to these new standards, and consultants across the country are hard at work facilitating teacher in-services on how to practice and evaluate close reading.

A chief concern that has prompted a surge in close reading and New Criticism professional development with the Common Core State Standards is misreading or how a reader's prior readings or experiences can interfere with comprehension. Reading within a community calls attention to I. A. Richards's concept of "mnemonic irrelevance," an interpretation unsupported by the text. Rosenblatt acknowledges that Richards's concern related to relying on readers' experiences to make the text come alive but suggests any potential problems are inevitable and even beneficial. She writes:

> Sometimes emphasis on the negative influence of the reader's personal concerns obscures their positive contribution. The reader's fund of relevant memories makes possible any reading at all. Without linkages with the past experiences and present interests of the reader, the work will not come alive for him, or, rather, he will not be prepared to bring it to life.
>
> (77)

Personal associations can explain why one student values a certain book and returns to it again and again. Tears, giggles, or a coiling gut are signs of a work's power over us. We do not want to deny a reader's right to such experiences. Yet readers do have a responsibility to determine how connotations drawn from personal memories are relevant to the reading experience, and here we see the value of reading in a social context: deliberation, which promotes consciousness. In other words, deliberation is the solution to the kinds of haphazard interpretations that Richards cautions us about.

The sympathy-eliciting function of narrative might mean the reader projects something out of her experiences that was only vaguely suggested by the text. While this might be considered a misreading of the text (but is still, perhaps, valuable to the reader's self), in the English classroom, there are other readers weighing in. It is the teacher's role to facilitate the discussion, to know her students and be responsive to their individual and social needs as they make and revise meaning. Community, therefore, heightens consciousness in our reading practices and mediates the memories that become integrated as new knowledge and experience.

Reading in a community can help ameliorate potential problems of misunderstanding and misinterpretation while allowing for alternate interpretations. As we saw in the previous chapters, people can interpret and manipulate words for their own purposes. How do we teach our students to navigate, negotiate, and participate as coagents of memory if they do not engage with one another in meaningful ways? If students consistently read within a community, they will benefit from the backgrounds, experiences, and intellectual and emotional responses of many. And they will learn to value one another at a time in their development that they are most interested in the self.

Aesthetic response makes possible a literary judgment and, according to Rosenblatt, "the honest recognition that one's own reaction is not in itself sufficient to ensure sound critical opinion" (72). The community and the recognition and respect for other judgments deepen our understanding of ourselves, others, and the text.

Space to Question the Narrative

During the class experience of reading *Tree Girl*, students were initially captivated by the narrative but became protective of their sympathies as the narrative unfolded. The spectacle of violence functioned as a catalyst for critique with very little guidance from me. The students' emotional responses—some they could articulate, but often there were emotions that I could not see nor could they name—elicited sympathy for the characters, which led to questions, critical conversations, and inquiry. Students were questioning the factors that may have influenced an author to create text; because they saw the text as something created, it was open to critique. For example, recognizing how a fictional account of genocide evokes such real sympathies for an imagined character, eighth-grade readers began to question the reliability of Mikaelsen's fictional Mayan narrator. The varied aesthetic responses to *Tree Girl* interacted with what students had learned about the structure of narrative and the features of genre. Mikaelsen, in the book's dedication, writes, "This book is dedicated to the real Tree Girl, who courageously shared her difficult story with me. She did so through many tears, from the protection of a safe house, during a long Guatemalan night. Her true experiences inspired this story." Whose narrative is at work here?

Recognizing the novel as historical fiction, students felt compelled to know the truth, to understand exactly what happened to Tree Girl and decipher "truth" and fiction. They wondered why "the real Tree Girl" could not write her story, which prompted discussions about *testimonio* and how authors mediating a subject's experience can enhance or detract from truth. In addition, students recognized the transactional nature of the nations depicted: Guatemala, the United States, and even Mexico acting and being acted upon because of social, political, and economic issues. Many of my students or their parents are from Mexico, and some crossed the border to the United States. We had long conversations about why there are no refugee camps at the U.S. border for Mexicans fleeing violence in their country. In fact, we followed this novel with a study of immigration to further explore the emerging questions. Our work had actually created more gaps than it filled.

Mikaelsen was a secondhand witness to these atrocities, listening to testimony of the real Tree Girl and rendering it for young-adult readers. The beautiful problem of historical fiction is that while readers learn *about* historical events, we are always wondering *what really happened and what was made up*. It is this wondering that prompts inquiry and critical thinking. In the case of *Tree Girl*, teen readers wonder:

- Why didn't the real Tree Girl tell her own story?
- Why did Mikaelsen choose to write a novel rather than a biography?
- Was Mikaelsen's account of the U.S., the Guatemalan army, the guerrillas, and the Mayans' role in the war biased?
- Why did Mikaelsen include such graphic details in some parts yet have the character turn away (thus not representing what happened) in other parts?
- What do authorial choices mean for representing atrocities in this genre and others?
- As a reader, should I turn away from the graphic content or read what he wrote? Am I exploiting the victims by reading it? Would my parents approve?
- Why might the novel's fictionality be important given that Tree Girl should not, in the name of genocide, have survived?

The multitude of voices that an author-secondhand witness can bring to the plane of the novel—the modern and ancient Maya, Spanish colonialism, rhetoric of war, American consumerism, refugees, grief—invites readers to ponder authorial choices, but as teenagers, as agents who will go on to tell about what happened and unveil other hidden atrocities, such literature appeals to their sense of justice and social agency.

Space for Inquiry

Questions about the School of the Americas, the Genocide Convention, and the massacre at Rio Negro led students to do more reading. Our classroom became a dynamic site of inquiry. We developed a wall of articles on various subjects related to Guatemala (e.g., the people, the culture, the food, the music, the art) and genocide (e.g., the Genocide Convention, the International Criminal Courts). I ordered books and DVDs from local libraries and created an online file with images and videos from my own travels to Guatemala. Students selected lines of inquiry that resonated, created research logs, and then were ready to synthesize their learning. A traditional research paper did not make sense in light of the way we were working. There was no linear way to capture what we were learning because while research filled some gaps, there were still more. I turned to Tom Romano's work in *Blending Genre, Altering Style: Writing Multigenre Papers:*

> A multigenre paper arises from research, experience, and imagination. It is not an interrupted, expository monolog nor a seamless narrative nor a collection of poems. A multigenre paper is composed of many genres

> and subgenres, each piece self-contained, making a point of its own, yet connected by theme or topic and sometimes by language, images, and content. In addition to many genres, a multigenre paper may also contain many voices, not just the author's. The trick is to make such a paper hang together.
>
> (xi)

So after a few days of research, students contemplated how best to make sense of what they learned—which genres could best capture their understanding of the topic—and then created their multigenre papers. Examples of their work follow.

On student, Jess, wanted to learn more about the refugee camps where Gabi lived after her cantón was burned down by government forces. She compared *Tree Girl's* depiction of the camps with articles about the living conditions of refugees, citing disease, death, scarcity of food, depression, and trauma. (See Figures 10.1 to 10.3.)

Inspired by the images of weaving I shared with students, Rachel viewed a Facebook page on Guatemala's weaving cooperatives, watched a video about backstrap weaving, and read a chapter from a book I found in my library on Guatemala to learn on how the symbols woven into the garments represent different aspects of the women's lives. (See Figures 10.4 to 10.6.)

Students turned their findings into new, original collections of texts for others to experience. We posted all these inquiry projects along the back wall of the classroom, and over several days students unpinned a project, took it to their seats, and read. Students were engaging in a multitude of transactions that were initiated because of aesthetic responses; without that real impact between the book and the reader, there would have been no process of meaning making to carry to the community. The transactions among the community were more productive and complex because students came with the necessary condition of judgment—an emotional reaction—and the recognition that their own reaction was not in itself sufficient to ensure sound critical opinion.

If students were to have read *Tree Girl* through standards-oriented methods, these transactions would have been more limited and controlled. For example, study guides and assessments that focus on vocabulary, character traits, symbol tracking, and comprehension limit the learning outcomes by constraining the reading event to just those objectives. Furthermore, the standards approach reinforces a view of literature as a means for teaching skills that exclude aesthetic responses, alternate interpretations, and further inquiry. One *Tree Girl* test that I found online (available for purchase) was a forty-question objective test, which included true/false questions, character-quotation matching, and sequencing events (Gall). The answer key was included. Reading *Tree Girl* to achieve a "right" answer or understanding of the novel and using an objective test to assess students' right reading would have made it easy for me to measure which students were "right" readers. However, I would have excluded the multitude of social actions that led to Jess and Rachel's multigenre papers.

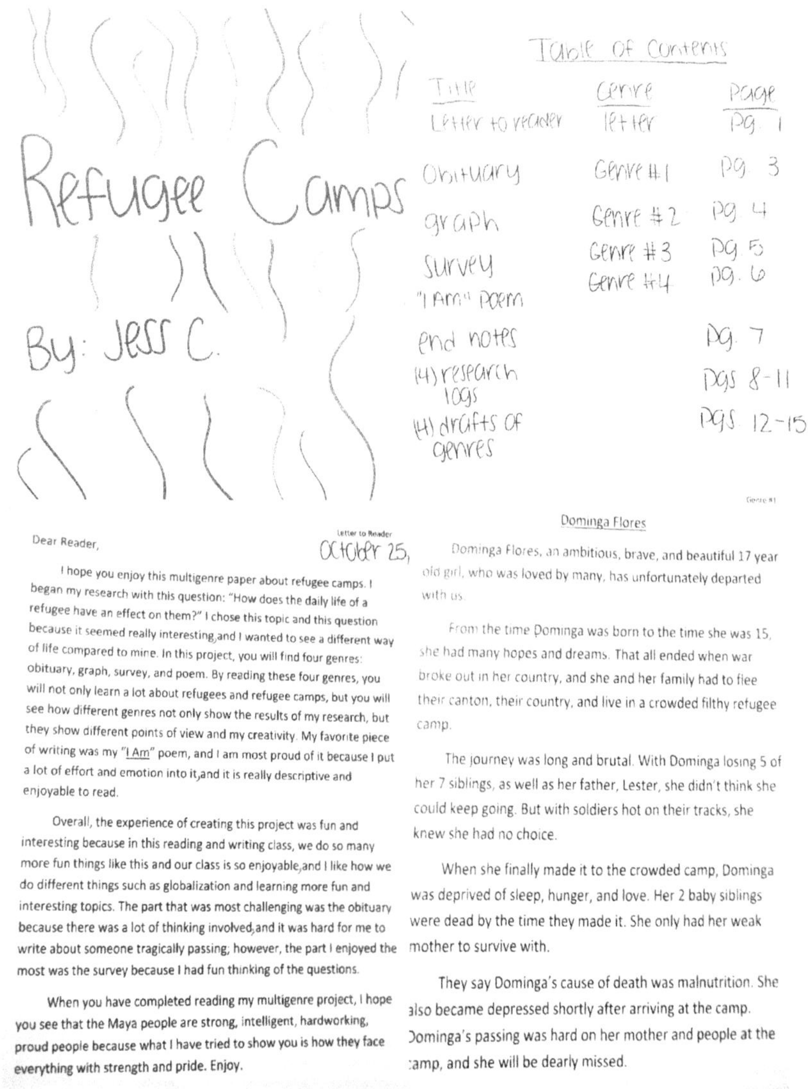

Refugee Camps

By: Jess C.

Table of Contents

Letter to Reader

October 25,

Dear Reader,

I hope you enjoy this multigenre paper about refugee camps. I began my research with this question: "How does the daily life of a refugee have an effect on them?" I chose this topic and this question because it seemed really interesting, and I wanted to see a different way of life compared to mine. In this project, you will find four genres: obituary, graph, survey, and poem. By reading these four genres, you will not only learn a lot about refugees and refugee camps, but you will see how different genres not only show the results of my research, but they show different points of view and my creativity. My favorite piece of writing was my "I Am" poem, and I am most proud of it because I put a lot of effort and emotion into it, and it is really descriptive and enjoyable to read.

Overall, the experience of creating this project was fun and interesting because in this reading and writing class, we do so many more fun things like this and our class is so enjoyable, and I like how we do different things such as globalization and learning more fun and interesting topics. The part that was most challenging was the obituary because there was a lot of thinking involved, and it was hard for me to write about someone tragically passing; however, the part I enjoyed the most was the survey because I had fun thinking of the questions.

When you have completed reading my multigenre project, I hope you see that the Maya people are strong, intelligent, hardworking, proud people because what I have tried to show you is how they face everything with strength and pride. Enjoy.

Genre #1

Dominga Flores

Dominga Flores, an ambitious, brave, and beautiful 17 year old girl, who was loved by many, has unfortunately departed with us.

From the time Dominga was born to the time she was 15, she had many hopes and dreams. That all ended when war broke out in her country, and she and her family had to flee their canton, their country, and live in a crowded filthy refugee camp.

The journey was long and brutal. With Dominga losing 5 of her 7 siblings, as well as her father, Lester, she didn't think she could keep going. But with soldiers hot on their tracks, she knew she had no choice.

When she finally made it to the crowded camp, Dominga was deprived of sleep, hunger, and love. Her 2 baby siblings were dead by the time they made it. She only had her weak mother to survive with.

They say Dominga's cause of death was malnutrition. She also became depressed shortly after arriving at the camp. Dominga's passing was hard on her mother and people at the camp, and she will be dearly missed.

Figure 10.1

Space Beyond the Classroom

University of Illinois at Chicago (UIC) hosts an annual Youth Development Summit. The summit supports youth-led social change and is an opportunity for youth development and community activists to come together, share their expertise, and learn from one another. In 2012, after reading *Tree Girl*,

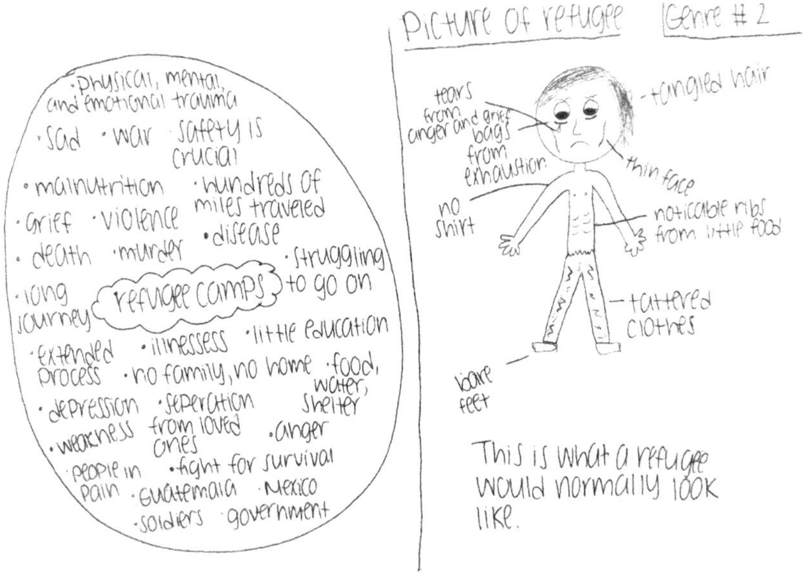

Figure 10.2

I told students about the summit and asked if they were interested in presenting. They wrote proposals to promote awareness of genocide, and four students were invited to speak at the Youth Voice in Action Summit. These students spent a week preparing for the presentation and organizing how best to uncover for their audience how they came to discover what genocide is and how it is impacting people around the world, specifically the Maya.

On the day of the presentation, the students discovered that they were the only middle school presenters—all the others were high schoolers. The audience knew they were witnessing something both remarkable and ordinary when one student, Mackenzie, whose family is from the Democratic Republic of Congo and who did his multigenre project on the Genocide Convention, explained that after WWII, the CIA created the School of the Americas in Panama. An excerpt from Mackenzie's presentation, in his own words, is below:

> In 1963, the School of Americas was relocated to Fort Benning, Georgia where 60,000 Latin American soldiers were trained in commando operations, sniper training, how to fire an M-16, and psychological warfare. Many U.S trained soldiers were found guilty of serious human rights violations and atrocities. What about the U.S. and the Genocide Convention? That was1948. Raphael Lemkin presented The Genocide Convention to prevent and punish genocide; the U.S. did not sign this

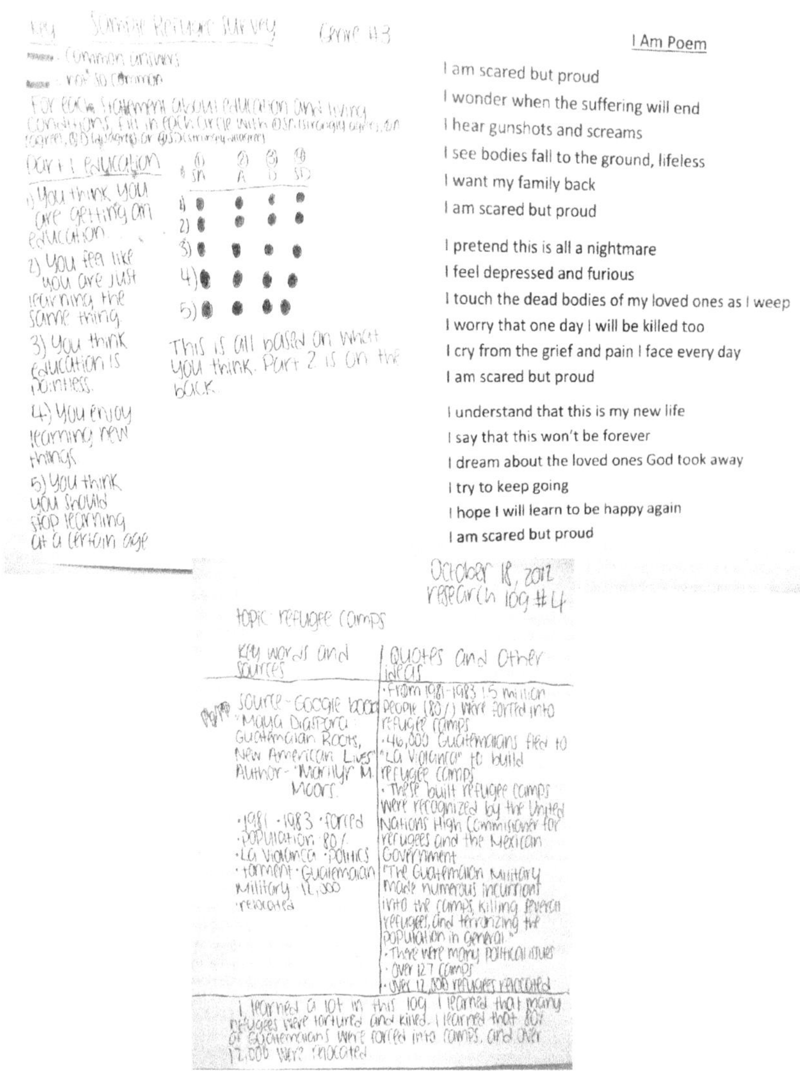

Key Sample Refugee Survey Genre #3

- Common answers
- not so common

For each statement about education and living conditions, fill in each circle with ① SA (strongly agree), ② A (agree), ③ D (disagree) or ④ SD (strongly disagree)

Part 1 Education

#	① SA	② A	③ D	④ SD
1)	●	●	●	●
2)	●	●	●	●
3)	●	●	●	●
4)	●	●	●	●
5)	●	●	●	●

1) You think you are getting an education.
2) You feel like you are just learning the same thing.
3) You think education is pointless.
4) You enjoy learning new things.
5) You think you should stop learning at a certain age

This is all based on what you think. Part 2 is on the back.

I Am Poem

I am scared but proud
I wonder when the suffering will end
I hear gunshots and screams
I see bodies fall to the ground, lifeless
I want my family back
I am scared but proud

I pretend this is all a nightmare
I feel depressed and furious
I touch the dead bodies of my loved ones as I weep
I worry that one day I will be killed too
I cry from the grief and pain I face every day
I am scared but proud

I understand that this is my new life
I say that this won't be forever
I dream about the loved ones God took away
I try to keep going
I hope I will learn to be happy again
I am scared but proud

October 18, 2012
research log #4

topic: refugee camps

Key words and sources	Quotes and other ideas
Source - Google book "Maya Diaspora: Guatemalan Roots, New American Lives" Author - "Marilyn M. Moors." ·1981 ·1983 ·forced ·population 80% ·La Violencia ·politics ·torment ·Guatemalan military 12,000 ·relocated	·From 1981–1983 1.5 million people (80%) were forced into refugee camps ·46,000 Guatemalans fled to "La Violencia" to build refugee camps ·These built refugee camps were recognized by the United Nations High Commissioner for refugees and the Mexican Government "The Guatemalan Military made numerous incursions into the camps, killing several refugees, and terrorizing the population in general." ·There were many political issues ·Over 127 camps ·Over 12,000 refugees relocated

I learned a lot in this log. I learned that many refugees were tortured and killed. I learned that 80% of Guatemalans were forced into camps, and over 12,000 were relocated

Figure 10.3

contract until the 1980s in part because of fear of being held accountable for crimes against humanity against Native Peoples of North America and slavery, but they ratified the Convention just after nearly 200,000 Mayans were massacred in Guatemala by soldiers they trained. You know, America is living in a bubble. And we have to pop that bubble. Don't be satisfied with easy answers. Ask questions, and then ask more questions. I was wondering, you know, about Columbus Day.

Mayan weaving is very interesting. Weaving is the woman and female children's job. Girls start weaving as young as eight or nine years old. They make their first piece of clothing at age eleven. Weaving is part of a women's daily life, and it is considered to be one of their main responsibilities. "Women communicate their social identity as well as their individual artistic creativity expressions through their weavings." (www.mayancolor.com)

A back-strap weaving loom is what many Mayans use to weave. They take the back rod and tie it to a tree or post, and the other strap goes around the weaver's waist. The loom has six sticks. A weaver usually sits on the ground, and they have a basket filled with scissors, balls of yarn, and a needle. The yarn is a plain color, and they die the yarn different ways to change the color. For example, brown yarn comes from a coconut shell, orange comes from carrots, soft yellow comes from chilca, and beige comes from the bark of an avocado tree.

Weaving is a very big part of the Mayan culture. For example, they pray to the gods that their daughters will be good weavers. Symbolism is very important in weaving. "Symbolism found in Mayan weavings is extraordinarily rich in heritage and culture which provides the weavers with a connection to their ancestors and traditions." (www.mayancolor.com) The designs on their weavings usually represent their life, the world they live in, their customs, traits, nature, and/or cosmology. The weavings are sold in markets across Guatemala. Therefore, Mayan weavings are extremely interesting.

Figure 10.4

I don't know if this offends you or anything, but it's kind of like we are celebrating genocide. So this brings up questions such as why we have school days off. Did Columbus actually discover anything? Didn't he bring about the death of many Natives? Let's think about all the post-Convention genocides. Obviously this did not work because so many

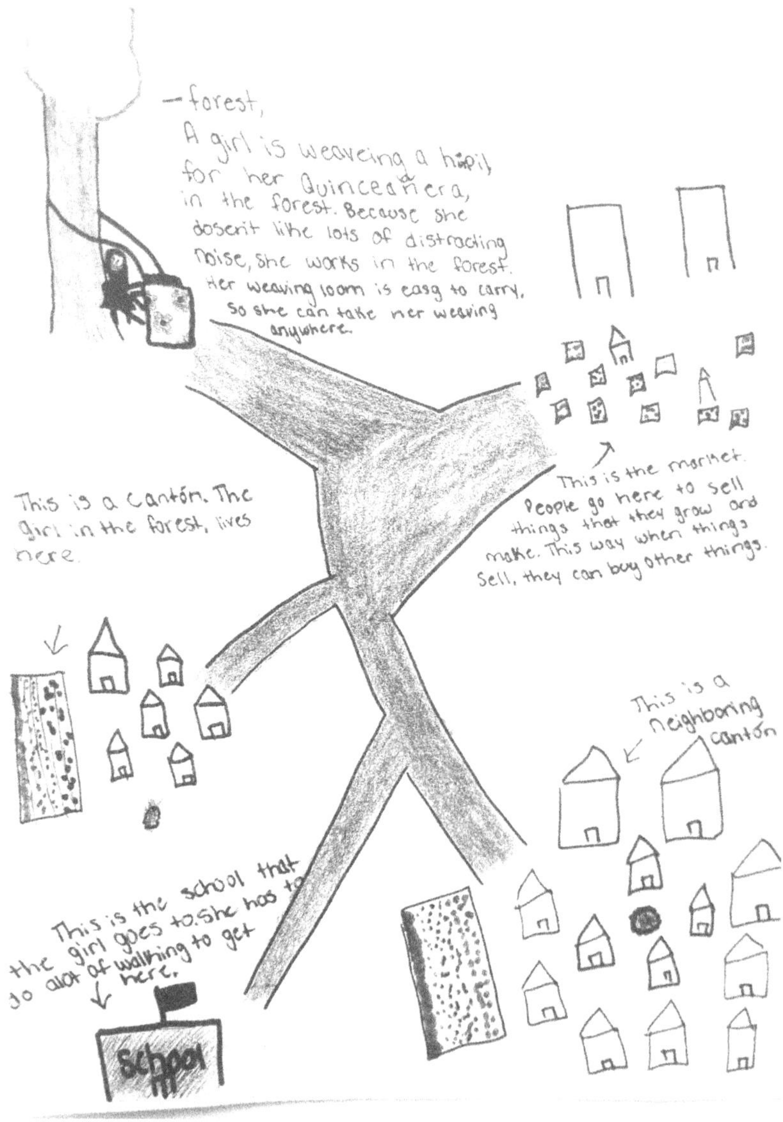

Figure 10.5

more genocides that have happened: Cambodia, Guatemala, Bosnia, Rwanda, Sudan. The list goes on—all terrible, terrible things. It saddens me. Like, why is this still happening?

For many audience members, this was the first they heard of the U.S. training and arming the Guatemalan military that killed more than 200,000 Maya in

We asked 100 Mayan women to take a survey and here are the results . . .

1) I like Weaving
   - ■ Yes
   - □ No
2) Weaving is a huge part of my daily life
   - ■ Yes
   - □ No
3) I was taught to weave at an extremely young age
   - ■ Yes
   - □ No
4) I am an extremely good weaver
   - ■ Yes
   - □ No
5) I use a back-strap weaving loom.
   - ■ Yes
   - □ No
6) My weaving represents my life, family, and culture.
   - ■ Yes
   - □ No
7) I do the same kind of weaving my ancestors did.
   - ■ Yes
   - □ No
8) When I weave, I have a basket full of scissors and yarn at my side.
   - ■ Yes
   - □ No
9) I make my own yarn, and I change the colors by using natural resources.
   - □ Yes
   - ■ No
10) Each string color stands for something in my culture or in my world
   - ■ Yes
   - □ No

Comments . .

Some of the comments were that weaving is the women's life. They are expected to make things to sell at the market, and to make clothes and household items for the family. They also have to cook and take care of the children.

I am calm and skilled
I wonder what the world would be like without weaving
I hear the sound of the yearn getting woven into a Hipil
I see the colorful yarn colors
I want to weave

I am calm and skilled
I pretend I'm not a weaver
I feel strings
I touch my loom
I worry about my loom getting lost or stolen
I cry when a string beaks

I am clam and skilled
I understand that each color string stands for something
I say I can weave beautiful things
I dream about weaving
I try to make money for my family
I hope my daughter will be a good weaver
I am calm and skilled

Endnotes

Source #1:
Title: Mayan Hands
Author: Mayan Hands
Copyright: N.D

I used this source in the first genre to learn about what the Mayan women weave. You learn about when Mayan girls start to weave.

Source #2:
Title: Back-Strap Weaving loom
Author: Education and More
Copyright: 2000–2012

I used this source to learn about the back-strap loom. I learned what it is and why the loom is used. I used this for the first genre and the second genre.

Source #3:
Title: Mayan weaving. A Living Tradition
Author: Ann Stalcup
Copyright: 1999

I used this source to learn about the weaving techniques, and how it affects Mayan culture. The weaving symbolizes nature, tradition, and culture. I used this for the first and third genre.

Source #4:
Title: Art of Weaving
Author: Maya color
Copyright: 2008

I used this source to learn about the back-strap weaving loom and more about how weaving is a part of Mayan culture. There are also symbols that stand for different things in a women's and girl's life. I used this in the first genre and the fourth genre.

Figure 10.6

the 1980s. Following is some dialogue from the question-and-answer session that followed the presentation:

AUDIENCE 1: What can be done?

AUDIENCE 2: For young people your age to already be talking about it, the idea that what this summit is about really understanding that the world is yours, you just have to go and do it; the fact that you guys are already connected to these concepts . . . and the idea again of making sure that you guys are developing that critical lens about that which most people don't talk about, but you guys are talking about it. When you become adults, you will be ready to challenge these things.

MACKENZIE: My parents when they were growing up, they were in their own little world and they learned what their teachers taught them. They learned whatever the curriculum was and they didn't know. Now they know, but in our generation it is hard to miss because it is all over the web and hard to miss. All of us here are involved with social media and stuff like that; for us, it is not hard to miss and it's hard to get out. We can't go around it; we have to go through it.

Later, the students were on a panel to debrief the summit. Following is an excerpt:

PANEL FACILITATOR: When you hear the term "youth voice," what does this term mean to you?

MACKENZIE: Actually, what it really means to me is it doesn't matter what age you are—me/us—we can speak our minds. Just because we're young, it doesn't mean we can't be a part of the change.

It was remarkable to hear how articulate these teens were, but it was ordinary in the sense that every student is capable of uncovering, preparing, and presenting research publicly. It should not have been so astonishing, and the fact that people were thinking this was so extraordinary, me included, is an indication that society needs to create more space for youth voices to be heard and for students to experience their role as agents of memory. The students' shared reading experiences contributed to their being able to demonstrate their ethical sympathy in this public space, beyond the classroom.

In the summer of 2012, I participated in Tulane University's Summer Teacher Institute on the Maya, "Signs of Change: A Glimpse of Past and Present Cultural Landscapes of Guatemala." I wanted to explore Guatemala and its geography, people, and culture. With archaeologists and local guides, we explored complex issues of identity, globalization, language, and cultural inheritance in Antigua, the highlands, and the rainforest. On this trip, we visited a school in Chimaltenango where the principal is a genocide survivor who, after escaping to Canada during the violence, has returned to his community to build a bilingual and bicultural school for children from two to six years old.

Project *Kaqchikel* (meaning "little sibling" in a native Mayan language) provides daily meals, healthcare, and education in both English and Kaqchikel. New reports suggest malnutrition leads to lifelong problems, and in Guatemala nearly 50 percent of the children are so malnourished that they are stunted physically and developmentally for life; they do not have access to foods beyond the staple: beans ("Widespread Childhood Malnutrition"). Education and humanitarian efforts seek to get proteins and vegetables to the highlands, but families still have to travel to sites down rough, unpaved roads. Even though the countryside is overflowing with fresh vegetables, very little makes it into local homes. It goes to export markets. Parents let their children go to Project Kaqchikel's My Melody School when they are young because the little ones get in the way or are an added burden on the backs of their mothers working in the fields. When they can be of use, children stop attending school to work. The principal is trying to build more classrooms and persuade parents to let at least one child stay in school, but the project of reviving Kaqchikel in Chimaltenango is dire. With the recent trend of unaccompanied *child* migrants arriving to the United States from Guatemala and other Central American countries because of violence, debates regarding immigration policy are shifting to refugee resettlement, according to the executive director of Kids in Need of Defense (KIND).

Gabriela, Jess, Rachel, and Mackenzie, along with their classmates, developed a multi-tiered fundraising campaign between October and December to sponsor a child at My Melody. They organized events to promote community at our school while raising funds for My Melody: tournaments for basketball, dodge ball, and video games; cookie baking and sale; and open mic nights.

Conclusion

Recognizing the rhetoricality of language means noticing the act, the intention of language to move others to think, believe, and act. Studying genocide is a *good* way to teach rhetoricality because the word "genocide" is such a powerful and consequential illustration of the ways in which "genocide" can mean different things depending on who is uttering the word, the speaker's purpose, and the historical context.

As we comply with the mandate to teach a unit on genocide or as we make changes in our curriculum to build knowledge, enlarge experience, and broaden worldviews, we can see this unit as one that can prepare students to ethically engage with international issues. They are already participants in their world, but with packaged curriculum, books as information vessels, and data measuring their value, students can see themselves as spectators—not at all directly involved by their watching or reading of texts and images that depict social issues.

The shift in education needs to come from the discipline of English, where we have a tradition of storytellers and translators always seeking alternative interpretations and diligently ruling out misinterpretations. The English classroom has to go beyond language as communication or as a means to transfer information; if rhetoricality is our condition, then our work must account for how every speaker, utterance, and situation that came before and after is transacting to represent not only a condition of human experience but actions that perpetuate disparate conditions. While rhetoricality is a quality of language, it is, more broadly, a condition of our human experience. Rhetoricality, like reader response, is still limited. There is a great deal of the human experience that is beyond knowing. How can students practice ethical reading—aesthetic reading and rhetorical reading?

The aim of reading genocide literature is not to just open students to the spectacle of atrocities in the classroom or to draw out sympathies. Rather, as Wendy Hesford suggests, the aim is to incite the potential for intelligent social action in response to the social needs revealed by our reading experiences. Such a move cannot happen when teachers and students expect logical, evaluative statements in response to reading rather than, as Misson and Morgon put it, more "immediate, inchoate, and emotional responses" (108).

Essentially, I see the pursuit of "college and career ready" and skills-oriented pedagogy as similar in the sense that quantifiable, measureable methods are all part of the standards, testing, progress regime, the aim of which seems to be achievement. For what are we preparing students, other than a grade, other than a test that decides if they are on the path to being "college and career" ready? What sort of human being is a college or career expecting? How should the English classroom be structured to reflect the values we want to see and experience in society? Current reading trends omit and constrict aspects of the reading process that I have shown to be vital areas of inquiry—like response, sympathy, responsibility, and activism—in favor of testing. The shift in pedagogy from skill-oriented methods to inclusive, rhetorical-oriented methods involves calling attention to how the text is constructed by encouraging literary discussions about the ethics of sympathy or emotional responses; it means reading within a community to make and revise meaning together; and it means taking those reading practices beyond the classroom to public spaces and ultimately to how we read social media, images, films, and the news and become responsible for our reading.

Works Cited

Bakhtin, Mikhail. *The Dialogic Imagination: Four Essays.* Austin: University of Texas Press, 1981. Print.

Boyles, Nancy. "Closing in on Close Reading." *Educational Leadership.* 70.4 (2012–13): 36–41.

French, Brigittine. *Maya Ethnolinguistic Identity: Violence, Cultural Rights, and Modernity in Highland Guatemala.* Tucson: University of Arizona Press, 2010. Print.

Gall, Angela. "*Tree Girl* by Ben Mikaelsen Test." *Teachers Pay Teachers.* 15 May 2016. Web.

Hesford, Wendy S. *Spectacular Rhetorics: Human Rights Visions, Recognitions, Feminisms.* Durham, NC: Duke University Press, 2011. Print.

Historical Clarification Commission. *Memory of Silence: Report of the Commission for Historical Clarification Conclusions and Recommendations*, 1999. AAAS.org. Web.

Kaplan, Brett Ashley. *Unwanted Beauty: Aesthetic Pleasure in Holocaust Representation.* Urbana: University of Illinois, 2007. Print.

Landsberg, Alison. *Prosthetic Memory: The Transformation of American Remembrance in the Age of Mass Culture.* New York: Columbia UP, 2004. Print.

Mikaelsen, Ben. *Tree Girl*. New York: Harper Tempest, 2004. Print.
Misson, Ray, and Wendy Morgan. *Critical Literacy and the Aesthetic: Transforming the English Classroom*. Urbana: NCTE, 2006. Print.
Richards, I. A. *Poetries and Sciences*. London: Routledge, 1970. Print.
Romano, Tom. *Blending Genre, Altering Style: Writing Multigenre Papers*. Portsmouth, NH: Heinemann, 2000. Print.
Rosenblatt, Louise. *Literature as Exploration*. New York: Appleton Century, 1938. 4th ed. New York: Modern Language Association, 1983. Print.
Weissman, Gary. *Fantasies of Witnessing: Postwar Efforts to Experience the Holocaust*. Ithaca, NY: Cornell UP, 2004. Print.
"Widespread childhood malnutrition is a paradox in agriculturally rich Guatemala." *PBS News Hour.* 25 June 2014. Web.

Literature for Your Classroom Library, Guatemala

Brown, Skila. *Caminar*. Somerville, MA: Candlewick Press, 2014. Print.
Cameron, Ann. *Colibri*. New York: Farrar, Straus and Giroux, 2003. Print.
Mikaelsen, Ben. *Red Midnight*. New York: HarperCollins Publishers, 2002. Print.
Mikaelsen, Ben. *Tree Girl*. New York: HarperTempest, 2004. Print.
Pellegrino, Marjorie W. *Journey of Dreams*. London: Frances Lincoln Children's Books, 2009. Print.
Reichs, Kathy. *Grave Secrets*. New York: Scribner, 2002. Print.

A Teacher's Testimony

Elaine Vogel taught middle school English for thirty-eight years. Here she reflects on reading genocide literature with her students and its impact on her practice over the years:

> When I first started teaching genocide, my focus was mainly on teaching facts. I wanted the students to learn who the victims and perpetrators were of the various genocides, the reasons behind them, and the outcomes. We read a lot of informational articles in packets as a part of our unit study.
>
> Then, we introduced genocide novels into the curriculum. Unfortunately, I still focused on learning the facts. Students got into groups to complete worksheets asking for the same information we focused on earlier—who, what, when, where, why and how of the genocides. I noticed that when the students got into groups to complete the fact sheets, they were also discussing how the atrocities affected the characters in the novels, they questioned the actions of the perpetrators, and they had strong reactions to what was happening in the novel. They

were connecting with the text on a much deeper level than what I was asking them to do. Eventually, I changed the group work to focus more on discussion and helping them gain a deeper understanding of what the victims living through the genocide experienced.

When deciding which novels to use for whole-class or small-group reading, I feel that I always chose books that exposed students to new ways of thinking, and/or helped them become more compassionate, empathetic individuals. After teaching genocide using novels, I really saw the impact the stories had on the students. They not only learned what happened during the genocides—the killing of families, the raping of the girls and women, and the destruction of towns and villages—but they were able to develop compassion toward the victims. They gained a better understanding of the horrors of genocide. In addition, they learned about life outside their worlds and developed an appreciation for what they have.

I think that using novels to teach genocide made me realize the impact books can have to change minds and hearts. When teaching the unit, I didn't focus on the literary elements and vocabulary development that I often focused on when teaching a novel. Instead, I focused on eliciting an emotional response from the students. I wanted them to fully understand the realities of injustice. Genocide wasn't only statistics and facts on a piece of paper, but was about people like us whose lives were devastated.

As a part of the unit, the students were given open-ended questions to respond to prior to meeting in their book groups. This gave them an opportunity to develop their own thoughts to bring to their groups. Their discussions were typically thoughtful and the discussions were lively. They had a much greater understanding of genocide than when we read facts and statistics from a packet. The students developed an empathy that could have only been achieved by focusing on the people affected by the devastation.

Overall, teaching genocide using novels was very effective and including open-ended questions and discussions was the key to the students' understanding.

11 The Reading Workshop

In the previous chapters, I've shared stories of my classroom. We read testimonial literature, *First They Killed My Father*, as a class (Chapter 9). We read a genocide novel as a class, *Tree Girl* (Chapter 10). However, genocide literature does not have to read exclusively as part of "unit of study." Students can read genocide literature in small groups when given the space to read as a community and do inquiry. In this chapter, I will show how teachers can take a step back from framing the book for students, leading discussions, and, overall, being an authority on the text.

The Reading Workshop

The year I spent minimizing worksheets and textbooks, I know that I came closer to being the teacher I imagined. I read those books with students because I know that literature and the many stories it tells can support one goal of the genocide mandate: "to deter indifference to crimes against humanity and human suffering wherever it may occur." However, in not creating an environment that honors student choice, I cannot say that I've witnessed students' capacity to seek out, stay with, ponder, and discuss the stories of our world on their own and beyond the classroom. What is the point of all this if students will not continue to read rhetorically and bear witness to lives after school, where we need them to intervene in injustice and innovate for a better world? Indeed, Mackenzie's presentation at the youth summit and the students' fundraising efforts to support the school in Guatemala are examples of social action that emerged from our study of genocide literature, but the structure of my classes was still fairly traditional. We read one book at a time with the occasional book group. I was making all the decisions, and we just weren't reading enough. Clearly, students were interested in what we were reading, but I felt like I was holding them back with the slow-paced whole-class novel. Three or more weeks to read a two hundred-page novel is just not how real readers read. I wondered how I could take all that I had learned about genocide and from genocide to the reading workshop model.

For the 2015–2016 school year, a decade after I helped write the genocide curriculum, I finally adjusted the structure of the classroom to be more aligned with the lessons of genocide. I wanted to bring student voices to the center of the classroom and take up my role as reader alongside them, just one more voice in our community of readers and thinkers. I made independent and small-group reading the priority with student choice and time to read. Three great resources for setting up and facilitating reading workshop are Donalyn Miller's *The Book Whisperer*, Penny Kittle's *Book Love*, and, of course, Nancie Atwell's *In the Middle.* Nancie Atwell writes, "Rather than relegating it to homework status, as a follow-up activity to the teacher's lectures, I make reading the central activity of the literature program" (157). Donalyn Miller's work connects what readers do in life to what readers do in school. She writes, "I am convinced that if we show students how to embrace reading as a lifelong pursuit and not just a collection of skills for school performance, we will be doing what I believe we have been charged to do: create readers" (4). And Penny Kittle's *Book Love* reminds us that a love of reading has to be cultivated in English class, and after a decade of NCLB, we have our work cut out for us.

The books we share with our students matter, but how we read those books matters more if we want students to read beyond the classroom. Genocide literature teaches us that beyond the classroom is where we need our students to be reading if they are to uncover and intervene in society.

Teach Reading and Literature *While* Students Read

Reading workshop is about making time for students to read. In a typical day at school, how much time do students spend reading? When the school day is over, students have sports, clubs, and sibling-sitting commitments. Some may read at home in the evening, but many do not, especially if there is no adult at home to encourage it or no quiet, well-lit space to invite it. Still, if the work of an English teacher is to teach students how to read and how to make sense of the written word, shouldn't we be available to students as they read? We make the most difference if we can be a resource to the entire reading process—from selecting to beginning to making meaning to looking back at the text as a whole. Teaching English is facilitating this process, which we can't do if we don't witness students reading and meaning making.

The reading workshop is about students gaining the capacity to read beyond the classroom. It is a way of organizing your classroom to support students in paying attention as they read, problem solving when stuck, finding books that are satisfying, and making and revising meaning.

We start class every day with quiet reading time. We typically set aside about fifteen minutes of independent reading time, but once a week, we read for thirty of our forty-one-minute class period. We will read two books together this year, but students will read between twenty and fifty (or more) on their own: long books, short books, different genres, different subjects, graphic novels, comic books, novels in verse, poetry, informational books, even some beautiful picture books. I have added to my library of genocide literature stories about immigration, books about ability and gender difference, books written by diverse authors recommended by We Need Diverse Books, and the latest young-adult novels recommended by Nerdy Book Club. I am reading constantly so that I can share books to "deter indifference to crimes against humanity and human suffering" within and beyond genocide. We have become a community of readers sharing books, uncovering what makes a "good" book, stretching our reading experiences beyond the familiar, and recognizing the ways authors use form and language to represent the world for readers.

Model Many Ways to Engage With and Respond to the Text

Part of reading workshop is offering a variety of ways to engage with a text and then encouraging them to select what works best for them. Throughout the year, we try literary letters, sticky notes, journaling, blogging, discussions, and drawing. I am, perhaps, overly careful about any practice that constrains or standardizes the experience of reading for students; however, I am an experienced reader who can support students as they figure out how to create, for themselves, positive, effective reading experiences. So I model what I do and invite other students to model what they do in the hopes that together we can figure out what works for everyone.

For me, I've always written in my books but especially in the back of the book, where I keep a list of characters, places, and page numbers. Students do not own the books they read in class, and some do not own any books at home, so I show them how to do this by putting large sticky notes in the back of the book. This method improves my comprehension without interrupting my reading flow, and students like this because it is easy to reference during discussion and just to remove and stick in their notebooks when they finish the book.

Nancie Atwell makes notebook letter writing central to her reading workshop. She explains to students, "In your letters talk with us about what you've read. Tell what you noticed. Tell what you felt and why. Tell what you liked and didn't and why. Tell how you read and why. Tell what these books said and meant to you" (193). She and her students respond to these letters as a way of building a community of readers, sharing books, and documenting learning. These do work well in notebook form or in blog form.

For the first quarter of this semester, students wrote letters once a week on their blogs and responded to their peers. They made claims about what big questions their books seem to be asking (e.g., what does it mean to be poor, what does it mean to be popular), and they made observations about how the setting impacted the plot or the function of supporting characters. They talked about how the story was moving them to feel and think about a subject in different ways and whether the story or ending was cliché or complicated expectations. One student, Rebecca, selected Linda Sue Park's *A Long Walk to Water* to read on her own. For a few days, I watched Rebecca work through this short but powerful story of Sudan in two time periods. Sometimes I'd see her write notes in her notebook, but I mostly saw her so captivated by the story that she only stopped when our reading time ended. Here is Rebecca's blog post:

> The title of the book I'm reading is *A Long Walk to Water*. The author is Linda Sue Park. Set in the 1980s and the 2000, in southern Sudan, there are two stories, but today I'm only going to talk about one. My character's name is Salva. He is trying to survive a war, traveling by foot trying to get out of the country for his own safety and protection.
>
> What I want to discuss this week is Salva's journey through the brutal conditions and pain, how he managed to survive so far. Salva started this journey when he was only 11 years old. The war drove him away from his family forcing him to travel with groups of people who treated him poorly because he was a child. For example in the text (pg. 66) it says "No one shared anything with him, neither food nor company. Salva had to beg for scraps which were given grudgingly. Salva managed to find his uncle weeks later." He manages to keep Salva safe for time being. Salva lost many loved ones through this journey, from being shot, to wild animals attacking them. This passage shows that Salva really struggled through this long journey of hate, blood, and anger. This is what I think of all of this: Salva manage to survive a life or death experiences, he can now manage anything.

I had the privilege of reading close to ninety of these each week. Sometimes I would respond to the blogs, and sometimes I would make a note to confer with the student the next day. Students also read and responded to each other, which helped build an online community of readers and stretch their "what's next" reading lists. Using blogs creates a portfolio of reading experiences where students can go to consider patterns and shifts in their learning, too. At the end of the quarter, I ask students to look through their reading notes and blogs and make sense of the way the texts are representing humanity and informing their views of the world.

Confer During Reading Time

I work my way around the room during quiet reading time. I do not call students over to my table because I feel like I am imposing my authority on them. When I sit or kneel alongside a student as she reads, I ask permission to chat. I am on my knees or pull up a chair into their space, asking for a glimpse into their reading experience. I also use this time to review what they wrote on their blog or talked about in their book groups. I make recommendations for books and talk about what they and I notice about the way the authors are representing the subject and characters for teen readers. This is where the real teaching happens—in these one-on-one moments—and this is also a time for teachers to just ask about their students' lives.

When I meet with students for daily reading conferences, I ask them questions about the words they are noticing, how the characters are interacting, what subjects or big questions the book is exploring, and how the book is appealing to them. There is no one protocol that I follow when conferring with students because each reader is unique. I try to start with a general question and then stay open to the conversation and where it goes. Each student brings her own reading and life experiences to the conversation, as do I. Here are some questions I pose to make explicit the principles of rhetorical reading:

- What is happening to you emotionally? What feels familiar and unfamiliar? How is the author moving you to feel pity or joy? How is the author trying to satisfy you as a reader? Is there a cliffhanger at the end of chapters? Suspense?
- What are the ethical considerations of the text? Is it a child or teen narrator, and if so, is she/he treated as the authority? Are there other, older characters that have to come in to save or advise the teen narrator? What is the purpose of the supporting characters? What seems cliché? Does the author rely on stereotypes? Is there something fresh or unexpected here?
- How is the author blending fact and fiction (rational appeal)? What are you learning about the subject? Does a character or event feel like a teaching device? Is the book overly didactic? What do you notice about the writing? Is the subject at the center, or is the story driving the book?

Trust the Process of Book Groups

Independent reading is the foundation of the reading workshop because it encourages and supports autonomy. However, interdependence supports community and acceptance. Book groups encourage interdependence among class members. Teachers organize book groups in different ways: all groups read the same novel; groups read different novels within a theme; and groups read different novels with no particular theme. In each instance, students must "come to discussions prepared," "draw on that preparation by referring to evidence . . . to probe and reflect on ideas under discussion," "pose questions that elicit elaboration and respond to others' questions and comments," and "acknowledge new information expressed by others and, when warranted, modify their own views" (Common Core State Standards for Speaking and Listening). (I quite like these new standards.)

To support students' preparations, I schedule a book group discussion day each week and help the groups decide how best to section their books for discussions. As students read in class, I monitor their pace and check in with them during our conferences so that everyone can be ready for the upcoming group discussion. I encourage sticky notes to mark different aspects of the text so that they can refer to them during our daily reading conferences and for book group discussion. These sticky notes also mark passages for text evidence (another standard) related to unfamiliar words, words or objects that repeat, places that evoke feelings (surprise, humor, shock, confusion, concern), and details about characters (personality, realizations, and interactions).

The day before the book group discussion, students decide which snacks they'll bring, and we look at their sticky notes so they can develop questions. I found that the most thoughtful discussions emerge when students write their own questions from the sticky notes, places in the text that they want to illuminate. Furthermore, citing text evidence is easier when the pages are marked. Students can easily flip through their book for passages to discuss, bringing their own reading experience to the table. I sometimes offer a discussion guide, which is fairly basic, focusing on rhetorical reading and several standards: provide an objective summary, cite textual evidence, trace a theme's development, and determine meaning of words and phrases as used in a text. In the past, I required role sheets, which are common in literature circles (e.g., discussion director, literary luminary, word watcher). However, I found the role sheets can minimize the probing, reflecting, and overall discussions because the goal becomes filling out the sheets. Book groups not only provide an opportunity for students to build community and analyze literature, they also offer authentic experiences of relating.

No Frontloading Necessary: Three Boys Read *Broken Memory: A Novel of Rwanda*

I include this chapter on reading workshop because I want to give teachers permission to trust students with reading genocide literature without them, which means without days of frontloading or lectures, without graphic organizers. In the reading workshop, students are free to choose their groups and their books; of course, I make recommendations and give book talks enticing students to stretch their reading experiences, but if you make available meaningful literature, students will, together, make meaning.

One group of boys, Daniel, David, and Johnny, read *Broken Memory: A Story of Rwanda* by Élisabeth Combres. *Broken Memory* focuses on how Rwanda lives with the trauma of genocide with flashbacks to the 1994 genocide, which are treated with sensitivity (i.e., not overly graphic). At the age of five, Emma was hiding behind a chair as her mother was murdered. After the murderers leave, Emma's mom says, "You must not die, Emma!" Emma wanders out of her town, and an old Hutu woman takes her in, hides her, and cares for her even after the war ends. About eight years later, when Rwanda establishes Gacaca courts to allow victims to face the perpetrators,

Emma's nightmares worsen. She befriends Ndoli, a torture victim who is re-traumatized with each year's commemoration of the genocide, and together they begin to heal with the help of an old man helping child survivors.

Constructing the "Geno" in Rwanda

In Rwanda, the words "Hutu" and "Tutsi" became polarizing symbols during the Belgian colonial period, which followed World War I. In the colonial days of Rwanda, the Belgians at once unified and divided individuals by naming some "Hutu" and others "Tutsi," a fictional classification that forced individuals to identify with groups that the state positioned to be at odds with one another. Because of the construction of an ethnic binary in the colonial days of Rwanda, there was no national identity of Rwandans when Rwanda was granted independence in 1962. In these circumstances, the history of ethnic inequality created conditions in which the fear of genocide was, paradoxically, deployed to incite genocide in the name of ethnic survival. In other words, the conditions were such that the different tribal groups were of the mind that "we have to kill them before they kill us."

Philip Gourevitch, in We *Wish to Inform You That Tomorrow We Will Be Killed with Our Families*, writes, "Power consists in the ability to make others inhabit your story of their reality—even, as is so often the case, when that story is written in their blood" (52). Gourevitch goes on to discuss the colonial history of Rwanda as evidence of this saying that when the Belgians arrived, they could hardly have pretended they were needed to bring order to Rwanda. Originally, Hutus and Tutsis were class-based classifying terms; social mobility was possible, and so one could be a Hutu and later become a Tutsi depending on labor and income. In the early 1930s, Belgium went about regimenting Rwandan society along ethnic lines, shifting the internal and structural power, effectively racializing the system of dominance by the Tutsi minority, who levied taxes against their Hutu neighbors. In 1933, Belgium issued ethnic identity cards making it impossible for Hutus to become Tutsis; labels could no longer be a class issue or an economic issue or even a blood issue because DNA was not available to establish these categories. The state classified citizens, writing on them and, thus, constructing the stage for "genos" and later genocide. But how did the state decide which class would be the more noble and which marginalized? According to Gourevitch, the Western aesthetics provided the criteria for classification, a seemingly ontological logic:

> [The Belgians] sought out those features of the existing civilization that fit their own ideas of mastery and subjugation and bent them to fit their purposes. . . . The scientists brought their measuring tapes and calipers, and they went about weighing Rwandans, measuring Rwandan cranial capacities, and conducting comparative analyses of the relative protuberance of Rwandan noses. Sure enough, the scientists found what

> they believed all along. Tutsis had "nobler," more "naturally," aristocratic dimensions than the "coarse" and "bestial" Hutus.
>
> (55–56)

Belgium went about "making legible," as James Scott might say in *Seeing Like a State: How Certain Schemes to Improve the Human Condition Have Failed*, Rwanda by creating a system of power where the Tutsis were indebted to Belgium for their position of power then forced through identification to aid Belgium in transforming the economy from subsistence and food crops to export crops, like coffee.

The Belgians' attempts to make legible the land and people of Rwanda set the stage for a series of genocides and political unrest. Thus, ironically, it is this scientific, modernist process of categorization that makes genocide possible in that categorizing defines those who are to be included or marginalized—even eliminated from the state. The Hutus were roughly 85 percent, and the Tutsis were about 14 percent. The Twa were the remaining percentage. (My naming and measuring here, I admit, feels like a violation of sorts.)

In 1957, a group of Hutu intellectuals argued for a Hutu state on the basis of majority rules, actually using the identification mechanism for their argument. Such was the logic of democracy of the time—"majority rule" defined in terms of ethnicity. The construction of the ethnic binary and desire for an ethnic state was the beginning of political violence between Hutu and Tutsis in Rwanda. Gourevitch calls this the "social revolution" of Hutus organizing a violent campaign against Tutsis using the rhetoric of democracy (majority rules). In 1962, Rwanda was granted independence, but not before the UN warned "that someday we will witness violent reactions on the part of the Tutsis" (61). Because the Belgians constructed a "superior" ethnicity of Tutsis, the Hutus resented and also feared the oppressive Tutsi rule. This fear of extermination was what ultimately led the Hutu extremists to appropriate symbols of genocide and destroy the entire Tutsi population in order to preserve Hutus' symbolic ethnic rights. In 1994, the massacre of 800,000 Rwandans took just 100 days. Gourevitch observes,

> The mass of participants in the practice massacres of the early 1990s may have taken little pleasure in obediently murdering their neighbors. Still, few refused, and assertive resistance was extremely rare. Killing Tutsis was a political tradition in postcolonial Rwanda; it brought people together.
>
> (96)

The case of Rwanda invited inquiry as to the epistemology (or how) of names and how that naming positioned people, who are ontologically the same, hierarchically with horrific consequences. The project of today's Rwanda is to replace multiple names (Hutu, Tutsi, and Twa) with one: Rwandan. Genocide does not end. The legacy of genocide persists as

Rwanda lives and relives the memory of genocide with each year's commemoration of the genocide.

Three seventh-grade boys read Combres's *Broken Memory: A Novel of Rwanda* without all of this background knowledge. They came to the text as readers and trusted the narrative to uncover what it could, knowing that the gaps and fissures asked them to do further inquiry. They did not need me to read it aloud or to tell them what happened. They are readers and do what readers do: make meaning.

In classes of more than thirty, I typically have eight book groups going at one time, so in order to listen to and assess the book discussions (and to plan future conferences), I put digital recorders out on each table. The recording was for me, so that I could be in eight places at once and for the students to later listen to their conversations and analyze how they were making meaning together, specifically, how their conversation clarified and modified their comprehension of the plot but also how the subject was represented by specific word choices and characters' interactions.

Here is a transcript of a twenty-minute discussion about the first half of *Broken Memory* among Daniel, David, and Johnny.

DANIEL: First, we have to write four sentences that summarize the first half of the book.

JOHNNY: Life is hard, especially when you're a little kid.

DANIEL: No, we're not going to do anything about the theme yet. Just summarize. The first part of the book is during the war. Emma witnesses the death of her mom.

JOHNNY: No, she doesn't.

DANIEL: Did she hear the death?

JOHNNY: Yes.

DANIEL: Then, she witnessed it.

DAVID: No. No. She covered her ears. She saw her mom's dead body.

DANIEL: She heard the men shout. She heard her mom's suffering.

Here we see how the boys are negotiating meaning. What does it mean to witness? Can you witness with your ears, or must you see? Why does this matter for Emma and her story? I was not there to ask these questions or guide the discussion, but I don't think I needed to be. They are working together but also with the text to make meaning.

DAVID: Okay, so we can say Emma "heard" her mom die. Okay, second sentence. She ran away to a nearby village.

JOHNNY: You know what's funny? Emma's name is "normal," but the other characters like Ndoli are. . .

DANIEL: Then, Emma finds an old lady. Muke. Mukechris. Let me see. (Looking into the text.) Where does it say? Okay, so Emma finds Mukecuru and lives with her.

DAVID: Till the war's over.
DANIEL: Also, Mukchris (sic) is a Hutu.
JOHNNY: No, she's the other one.
DANIEL: No, Emma's a Tutsi.
JOHNNY: Oh, yeah.
DANIEL: And right now the war is between the Hutus and Tutsis.

If this book were framed as a genocide novel (part of a unit of study), then the students would have been focusing on this first rather than on Emma, I imagine. The fact that Emma is a Tutsi and Mukecuru is a Hutu is important, but these boys see Emma and Mukecuru as representing two human beings rather than two sides of a war or genocide.

DAVID: What's the third most important thing? Um, Emma discovered the boy, Ndoli.
JOHNNY: Wait, shouldn't we write about how her mother said what she wanted before she died?
DAVID: Yea, keep on living.
DANIEL: Right. Let's add that here. Mom told Emma not to die.

Johnny is reminding the group of a phrase that comes up again and again in this novel. Emma can hear her mom's voice, but she cannot remember what her mother looks like, and she is so haunted by her past that she cannot live fully in the present.

DAVID: What's the last sentence? Emma found a Tutsi who also went through the war?
DANIEL: Yea, he was tortured for information. He got his head beat in.
JOHNNY: That is what you call a Superman. He got hit by a machete and still survived.
DANIEL: And what's the most recent thing we read? [Emma] is about to go look for the old man? Emma like saw Ndoli and the old man under a tree. Okay, so now let's find some words.

Ndoli and the old man are important to the story because the old man was sent to the village to help people with PTSD, although they never call it that. The boys have only read the first half of the book, but this shows me that they understand what is going on and are ready for the next part of the story. In this next segment, the boys start talking about words that were unfamiliar or seemed important as they read.

DAVID: Silhouette.
JOHNNY: How about torrential?
DANIEL: Silhouette is like a shadow.
DAVID: Rwanda.

JOHNNY: So how do we spell. S-i-h-o. What page?
DANIEL: Page 67.
JOHNNY: What does it mean?
DANIEL: It's means like a shadow or a figure. No, wait it's a person. You can't really see any of the features.
DAVID: "I came around the bend in a cloud of brown dust with a hazy pink silhouette . . ."
DANIEL: So you can't see them, but you can see their figure and maybe the color of their skin.

The boys are reading a sentence from a scene in which a truck of men dressed in pink prison uniforms has arrived in Emma's village for the Gacaca courts, controversial community courts Rwanda established to deal with a backlog of cases of people accused of involvement with the genocide. In a public hearing under a tree, survivors could face the accused and give evidence.

JOHNNY: So the shadow?
DANIEL: Not shadow. It's actually the person.
JOHNNY: I don't get it. Why do they wear the pink?
DANIEL: It said something about the prisoners that they wore a shade of pink.
JOHNNY: Who has another word? I have like two more, but I don't understand them at all.
DAVID: I have tr. Trab.
DANIEL: Let me see. Tribunal? What page is this? You read it on the 26th, so it must have been early in the book. You got this, David, you can find it.

I love hearing the encouragement among the boys as they look for the pages and reread the words in context, but what's even more remarkable is that they are pointing out words that many teachers may have pretaught to prepare students to read. Here we see that given time and each other, the students can work with the text to uncover the meaning of words and how they construct an understanding of the situation represented (no teacher required).

DAVID: I have another one Gacaca. Gacaca. Gacaca court. Page 67. I just want to say Gacaca. City? "Emma heard they'd be coming back but first they had to . . . prisoners into the city. Present them to the community. Now they came . . .
(negotiating the pronunciation)
DANIEL: Yeah, that's not a thing. That's a place.

This is one part in the discussion that I want to come back to with the boys in our next conference. I think they get what is going on, but I am not sure if they are making the connection between the setting and its impact on

Emma. That said, the next part of the book will answer those questions, so I had to decide if I would intrude or not. I did.

DAVID: Commemoration. I don't know what page.
DANIEL: Oh my, David! Why aren't your sticky notes in the book?
JOHNNY: Can we do scrawny? Page 51.
DANIEL: Yeah, we can do scrawny.
DAVID: All skin and bones.
DANIEL: We need some context clues.
JOHNNY: "The shy, scrawny boy seemed almost invisible." So skinny. Almost invisible.
DANIEL: Definition: someone small, weak. Okay, so supporting characters. Ndoli. We can say he's the love interest.
DAVID: He is?
DANIEL: She describes him as beautiful. He sat there and he cared for her while she was passed out. In almost every story, there's a love interest, and who else do you think that will be? The old man?
DAVID: I feel like he is a five-year-old. That's what I feel like he is.
JOHNNY: So you think he joined the rebels at age five?
DANIEL: No, he's a teenager. He was being tortured, and if he said anything, he'd bring harm to his village. He's the love interest and mysterious character . . . Wait, how do you picture Ndoli?
JOHNNY: Skinny and bent over.
DANIEL: I imagine his head sort of like an alien shape. Dented on one side. His eyes are super bloodshot. And he is really skinny and scrawny. He wears raggedy clothes that are too big for him.
DAVID: I picture him small.

David, Daniel, and Johnny wrap up their discussion at this point. Daniel starts singing, "Feel the rain on your skin. No one else can feel it for you." Johnny and David decide it's time to turn off the recorder. In the last few utterances of their discussion, however, they are noticing how Combres has depicted Ndoli as stuck in the past, as still haunted by how he survived torture in betraying his family and other rebels. Ndoli's trauma is visible while Emma's is invisible, and Ndoli and Emma do support each other as their past arrives in trucks, dressed in pink.

This artifact offers evidence of students' discussion skills, an artifact for students to listen to, analyze, and improve upon for next time. Also, it is a form of assessment that honors a strength of many of our students, which is verbal communication. I met with David, Johnny, and Daniel the next class period to check in with them about the ideas they were negotiating during the discussion. Specifically, I talked about the word "silhouette," and how that word was illuminating a theme in the book but also in Rwanda as the country continues to heal. I encouraged the boys to research the Gacaca courts and come back to the word "tribunal," which was almost mentioned and overlooked. I also asked about what they were noticing about Emma's mental and physical health. Emma was having nightmares and isolating herself from her peers. I suggested students research PTSD and its treatment. The boys did some research and posted their findings on their blogs:

JOHNNY: What I want to talk about why those accused for genocide were wearing pink when the truck passed the village. Here is an article I read: "Forgiving Genocide."They wear pink because it represents how their trial is going. If it is pink, it means they don't have a sentence yet; if they wear orange, it means their case is done. One thing I got intrigued that wasn't in the book is why did it take so long to accuse them for the genocide?

DANIEL: I read an article from the *National Institute of Mental Health*. On one hand, what is similar to my book titled *Broken Memory* is that my main character Emma experienced a situation that has caused people to get PTSD. Emma witnessed her mom die, and Emma probably has PTSD because she has nightmare. When she heard the voice of the man that killed her mom when the gacaca courts started, she again freaked out. On the other hand, Emma was never told that she has PTSD, so I think she will be told soon, most likely by the old man who was helping Ndoli. He said he could "get rid of the nightmares."What I think about this is that you have to be really brave to live with PTSD.

The transcript and the follow-up blogs are so rich with meaning making. To assess reading, we have to really consider the process rather than a product or outcome. Recorded discussions offer students and teachers an alternative to testing. Students can upload an audio file to their blog as evidence of thinking and making meaning that is difficult to capture in a written assignment or test. After several book discussions, students can reflect on the development of their speaking and listening skills over time.

Reading workshop does require planning and coordination to be able to get to the point at which students are having these meaning discussions about literature, but what makes possible such thoughtful work is the daily practice of reading alongside other readers.

Conclusion

Teacher–student relations are bound up in inequalities, but the reading workshop positions the reader and the practice of reading at the center of the classroom. With a balance of whole-class, small-group, and independent reading experiences, all students can develop the capacity to not only read deeply but to select, discuss, and critique texts for how they are created and how they work on readers to see the world. The book choices, sticky notes, blogs, conferences, journals, research, and book group discussions make the English classroom a community space that nurtures readers and cultivates habits of reading and thinking that can extend beyond the classroom. The standards do not need to be used to standardize our students' thinking; students naturally defy such intentions. Create authentic reading experiences and use class time to be a coreader. You do not have to be the expert, and you don't need to frontload. Let the literature invite students into the narrative, and in the gaps and fissures, students will make meaning.

Works Cited

Atwell, Nancie. *In the Middle: Writing, Reading, and Learning with Adolescents.* Upper Montclair, NJ: Boynton/Cook, 1987. Print.

Combres, Élisabeth, Shelley Tanaka, and Michael Solomon. *Broken Memory: A Novel of Rwanda.* Toronto: Groundwood Books/House of Anansi Press, 2009. Print.

Gourevitch, Philip. *We Wish to Inform You That Tomorrow We Will Be Killed With Our Families: Stories from Rwanda.* New York: Farrar, Straus, and Giroux, 1998. Print.

Kittle, Penny. *Book Love: Developing Depth, Stamina, and Passion in Adolescent Readers.* Portsmouth, NH: Heinemann, 2013. Print.

Miller, Donalyn, and Jeff Anderson. *The Book Whisperer: Awakening the Inner Reader in Every Child.* San Francisco, CA: Jossey-Bass, 2009. Print.

"Preparing America's Students for Success." *Common Core State Standards Initiative.* 15 May 2016. Web.

Scott, James C. *Seeing Like a State: How Certain Schemes to Improve the Human Condition Have Failed.* New Haven, CT: Yale University Press, 1998. Print.

Literature for Your Classroom Library

Sudan

Bassoff, Leah, and Laura DeLuca. *Lost Girl Found.* Toronto: Groundwood Books/House of Anansi Press, 2014. Print.

Farish, Terry. *The Good Braider: A Novel.* Las Vegas, NV: Amazon Children's Pub, 2012. Print.

Mead, Alice. *Year of No Rain.* New York: Farrar, Straus and Giroux, 2003. Print.

Park, Linda S. *A Long Walk to Water: Based on a True Story.* Boston: Clarion Books, 2010. Print.

Pinkney, Andrea D., and Shane Evans. *The Red Pencil.* New York: Little, Brown and Company, 2014. Print.

Rwanda and Burundi

Carr, Rosamond H., and Ann H. Halsey. *Land of a Thousand Hills: My Life in Rwanda.* New York: Viking, 1999. Print.

Cornwell, Nicki, and Karin Littlewood. *Christophe's Story.* London: Frances Lincoln Children's, 2011. Print.

Jansen, Hanna. *Over a Thousand Hills I Walk with You.* Minneapolis, MN: Carolrhoda Books, 2006. Print.

Kidder, Tracy. *Strength in What Remains.* New York: Random House, 2009. Print.

Stassen, Jean-Philippe. *Deogratias, a Tale of Rwanda.* New York: First Second, 2006. Print.

Iraqi Kurds

Ellis, Deborah. *Children of War: Voices of Iraqi Refugees.* Toronto: Groundwood Books, 2008. Print.

Laird, Elizabeth. *Kiss the Dust.* New York: Dutton Children's Books, 1992. Print.

Robinson, Anthony, Annemarie Young, and June Allan. *Mohammed's Journey: A Refugee Diary.* London: Frances Lincoln Children's, 2009. Print.

Middle Passage

Anderson, M. T. *The Astonishing Life of Octavian Nothing, Traitor to the Nation: 1.* Cambridge, MA: Candlewick Press, 2006. Print.

Draper, Sharon M. *Copper Sun.* New York: Athenaeum Books for Young Readers, 2006. Print.

Fox, Paula, and Eros Keith. *The Slave Dancer: A Novel.* Scarsdale, NY: Bradbury Press, 1973. Print.

Grifalconi, Ann, and Kadir Nelson. *The Village That Vanished.* New York: Dial Books for Young Readers, 2002. Print.

Hendry, Frances M. *Chains.* Oxford: Oxford University Press, 2004. Print.

Ukraine

Dimarov, Anatoliĭ, Roma Z. Franko, Sonia V. Morris, Olena Zvychaĭna, Vasiliĭ Grossman, Robert Chandler, Elizabeth Chandler, and Anna Aslanyan. *Everything Flows.* New York: New York Review Books, 2009. Print.

Dimarov, Anatoliy, Yevhen Hutsalo, Olena Zvychayna, Sonia Morris, and Roma Franko. *A Hunger Most Cruel: The Human Face of the 1932-1933 Terror-Famine in Soviet Ukraine.* Saskatoon, SK: Language Lanterns Publications, 2002. Print.

Mak, Ol'ha. *Stones Under the Scythe.* Bloomington, IN: iUniverse Inc., 2011. Print.

Skrypuch, Marsha F., and Michael Martchenko. *Enough.* Toronto: Fitzhenry & Whiteside, 2000. Print.

Watts, Irene N. *Touched by Fire.* Toronto: Tundra Books, 2013. Print.

A Teacher's Testimony

Sumer Samano is a teacher in a suburb of Chicago. She was a student in my reading methods course at the University of Illinois at Chicago while I was working on my doctorate and she was earning a bachelor's degree in English education. A few months ago, she wrote me a letter. With her permission, I share it here:

> After trying my best to avoid any interactions with genocide literature—having to learn about it, being required to teach it, and cringing at the thought of it—I think I may finally be comfortable with it. A couple

of weeks ago, as I was scrolling through my news feed, I passed by videos and written reports on the damage and casualties happening back home. I felt a sudden burst of anger at the thought of how this situation isn't being dealt with ideally. I questioned why "they" weren't helping and before I could try to answer my own question, all that you do had finally hit me, "*This* is why Sarah does what she does . . ." followed by a solid minute of just letting it all sink in and truly accepting it.

Last week, my school invited the same guest speaker they have had visit for a few years. He is a "Lost Boy," originally from Sudan. He spoke about his experience growing up and trying to survive as a refugee among the surrounding countries, dealing with daily extreme violence, deaths of family and friends, and starting a new life in the U.S. It was a fulfilling conversation; students asked insightful questions, and he was willing to share his whole life as a Lost Boy with everyone. My eyes continued to widen throughout this discussion with every experience he shared—I was rediscovering and confirming my realization of the purpose of your work. After the kids were dismissed, we briefly chatted and I asked him what I had been wanting to ask him since he started speaking, what could we do here for the folks overseas going through this besides trying to bring relatives/people over or sending money? Without hesitation, he said, "the best thing to do is to tell their stories." To clarify, I asked if he meant to bring awareness and he simply said, yes. We continued to talk about what comes out of telling their stories. By telling his story, he was able to receive the support to build and start up a school in his home village. Friends of his have started organizations here, in the U.S., to support those who have been affected by the wars in their homeland. This conversation evidently led to another, yet, more deep rooted, "this is why Sarah does what she does" realization.

My point in sharing this epiphany with you is that I know I have always been way too sensitive to truly acknowledge your activism. Although it's terrible, it took having to be a part of a community dealing with genocide to be able to recognize, understand, and to finally be somewhat involved in attempting to bring some good and peace to humanity. I always knew that what you do is bringing change for the better, but I am now beginning to understand that I wasn't able to process it or make the connections then—it was merely a surface level of understanding; I now see more. Hugs to you and people like you who have the motivation and compassion to make the changes we need; who knows where we would be now without you.

12 Assessment

No More Numbers and Letters

Sherman Alexie's novel *The Absolutely True Diary of a Part-Time Indian* is narrated by a fourteen-year-old Indian who is observant, clever, funny, and an artist. (I use "Indian" here to refer to Native Peoples of North America because Alexie does in his title.) Arnold Spirit Jr. narrates the year he made the choice to go beyond the boundaries of his reservation, "rez," to attend a white school twenty-two miles off the reservation, away from the only life he knows. The kids on the rez brand him as a traitor, and this tension cracks open the fissures of narratives of identity and belonging. I include Alexie's novel in this book about genocide literature because while it is a book about a boy leaving the reservation for a "better" life, it is a story that exists today because of genocide, because of systematic efforts to assimilate Native peoples into an emerging European American culture, and because Arnold Spirit Jr.'s story is a story of genocide's ever-lasting implications.

But this chapter is not a close reading of Alexie's novel. Indeed, I offer a glimpse of my experience reading it with eighth-grade students, but this chapter is about one more lesson I learned from reading genocide literature with young people. That is the need to not only read about systems that perpetuate crimes against humanity but to intervene and change systems that categorize and measure people.

Education in *The Absolutely True Diary of a Part-Time Indian*

Of particular interest to eighth-grade students when reading Alexie's novel was this passage about a teacher: "Of course, I was suspended from school after I smashed Mr. P. in the face, even though it was a complete accident" (31). What's not interesting about a student throwing a book at a teacher? However, what was even more surprising to students was when Mr. P., the white teacher who lived in the teachers' compound on the reservation, came to Arnold's house to apologize *to Arnold*.

Mr. P. explained that when he first started teaching on the reservation, the teachers were "supposed to kill the Indian to save the child." Mr. P. says, "We were supposed to make you give up being Indian. Your songs and stories and language and dancing. Everything. We weren't trying to kill Indian people. We were trying to kill Indian culture" (35). Students' responses to this passage were not too different from my own. While some students were imagining teachers trying to kill the Mexican in them or the Ukrainian in them by ignoring their language or culture, I was imagining the already vanished Italian in me. I had lost my culture in just two generations, and yet I perhaps had something else because of it (a life my grandfather, who came to America in 1920 with no job or education, could only imagine). Some students shared stories of their elementary teachers punishing them for speaking Spanish in class. Others said that while they could understand Spanish, they could no longer speak it, and this frustrated their parents. How do schools kill culture? Is it explicit? Are schools trying to standardize or make just one culture? If so, what are the implications?

While Mr. P. and Arnold were just two voices on the page, a multitude of discourses beyond the words on the page made this passage possible: an Indigenous author extremely conscious of his identity (Alexie), a history of colonization and genocide, the boarding school era, contemporary education on reservations, and the lives of readers. The Mr. P. chapter moved students to add "reservation schools" to their inquiry list, a list students keep in their notebooks for future research. They wanted to know more about the history behind "kill the Indian, save the child."

Students were asking about something that started way before Mr. P., namely the boarding school era. During an inquiry day, a day when students are free to research topics from their reading, one student found a clip from a television series about the boarding school era. It was from *Into the West*, a 2005 miniseries produced by Steven Spielberg that weaves real and fictional characters and events to represent the period of the United States expansion westward from 1825 to 1890. We took a look at Episode Five, which portrays an 1879 experimental school in Pennsylvania designed to "kill the Indian, save the child," the Carlisle Indian Industrial School. Eighth-grade Lincoln students watched Lakota children learning the "white man's ways." In the excerpt, Lakota children are forced to choose a white name, dress in the white man's garb, and allow a white man to cut their hair. One boy, Voices That Carry, resists. The headmaster says, "An Indian man only cuts his hair in a time of great mourning." Voices That Carry tries to escape but is caught; he sits on the ground; takes out his own knife and cuts his hair himself. He cuts his hair not because it is the white man's way but because he is in mourning for his people.

The cultural assimilation of Native peoples was a systematic process by the United States to transform Native culture to European-American culture between the years 1780 and 1920, an effort to standardize cultural values and practices, outlawing traditional religious ceremonies and establishing boarding schools; thus, education was the primary method of this process. This lesson on education in *The Absolutely True Diary of a Part-Time Indian* was not lost on the eighth-grade readers that day. Alexie's treatment of education is unflinching, which is why so many students love this book. Schools work to assimilate students to a certain set of values and beliefs about society. Instead of being a place that nurtures individuals and celebrates innovation, reform measures have been working within an exclusionary framework. One of the most obvious ways we categorize and make decisions about students is in grading practices.

Standards Not Standardization

We are teaching in a time of standards and standardization. I have referenced learning standards throughout this book, written descriptions of what students are expected to know and be able to do at a certain stage of their education. Teachers use these standards to guide instruction, assessment, and curricula, and schools may refer to this as standards-based instruction. However, we do not want to repeat the NCLB era of grouping students to target for skills-based instruction. The new standards descriptions give teachers freedom to choose the content and method for the lives and academic needs of the students with whom we share the classroom. And because there is nothing in the standards to indicate how teachers should assess learning, teachers can choose that, too. Traditionally, teachers have assigned a number or letter to assignments and projects, but these are measurements that cannot capture the complexity of learning. Consider the discussion on *Broken Memory* in Chapter 11. Here, I recommend a more humane, nuanced assessment practice that minimizes the use of scores and letter grades to assess learning in an effort to ward off standardization.

In this book, I have discussed how high-stakes testing has narrowed reading approaches and minimized students' voices in their learning, but up until now I have yet to address one of the more oppressive practices in schools, one that does not align well with the rhetoricality, witnessing, and social action, and that is grading. In all my efforts to make space for complexity and nuance in the classroom with multigenre projects, memoirs, and public speaking, I still marked up glorious artifacts of learning with that red pen. (Actually, I'd used green or purple pens, fooling myself into thinking they'd be less oppressive.) Rhetoricality and witnessing represent important shifts in how I teach reading and literature because learning and expression of learning became social actions in the classroom and beyond—for students and for me. However, this school year, I thought: What is the point of this shift in pedagogy if I do not shift my approach to assessment? How could I use the standards to guide instruction without standardizing the thinking of students? Thus, the most important action I have taken yet in my teaching practices came this year when I began minimizing scores and grades in my classroom.

The Darker Side of Numbers and Letters

The incident that prompted my shift in grading was the spring term the previous school year. Our administrators alerted the teachers to a disturbing trend that had been building, which was overlooked for some weeks because of the high-stakes testing window in the spring: low GPAs. Quite a few eighth-grade students were in danger of not being able to attend their graduation ceremony because their GPAs were below the required 1.0.

Teachers were charged with the task of "targeting" students with low GPAs, a task that the administrators had previously managed with grade contracts, after-school work sessions, and parent meetings. The time and energy spent in team and faculty meetings and over emails talking about low-GPA students was staggering, and while the list led to conversations about often-marginalized students, the conversations also pointed out problems with grading, zeros, homework, late work, rubrics, and absences. The conversation, however, did not lead to any school-wide shifts in grading or scoring practices, in part because we were in the midst of two rounds of PARCC testing and in part because the rhetoric of grades and the system of ranking students according to grades *is* school for so many teachers. Still, the whispers in my conscience about the ethics of grading were getting louder.

Without grades, what would motivate students? Might students go beyond compliance toward greater engagement and involvement in their learning? How would students and teachers recognize and celebrate learning and discoveries? What might students discover about themselves, learning, school, and the world? And how might the conversations among teachers and administrators change?

Clearly, these are broad questions, and minimizing grades is a great undertaking requiring cooperation from many teachers and administrators, but I asked my principal if I could give it a try and proposed a "no-grades classroom" to pilot for the next school year. (Starr Sackstein included my story in her book *Hacking Assessment: 10 Ways to Go Gradeless in a Traditional Grades School*.) Of course, many teachers in our school already resist grades by not putting a grade on everything, by doing more conferencing, by weighting results over process in their grade book. However, I was not convinced that outcomes or products should be the goal. Learning is a process that is ongoing, so to put a score on that at any point seemed counterintuitive. A shift in assessment practices would require a shift in the language we used to talk about learning.

Is This for a Grade?

If the assignment is not for a grade or not for points, what is it for? In the final weeks of the school year, I searched for resources to help me work through this question. *Assessment 3.0* by Mark Barnes offers many helpful suggestions and a strong argument for implementing a no-grades classroom and school (and then you feel like you can phase out, invalidate, eradicate, or "throw out" those grades). Barnes argues: "Eliminating traditional grades is not only possible but is, in fact, necessary if we are to evolve beyond the archaic measurements that stifle learning" (4).

Why do this when it is not school policy or when we still have to enter midterms and report card grades? Barnes says, "You just do it because our greatest responsibility is to kids" (6). Perhaps the teacher next door will use grades, and it is likely that the teacher in the next grade will use grades, but it is not a good enough reason to abandon what is "right" for the human beings with whom we are entrusted. As I have been suggesting, teachers are part of the institution, and we have a responsibility to shape its structures in ethical ways.

Barnes suggests grades "stunt" the growth of our students. Even if we provide narrative feedback, if we also assign a grade, "students ignore comments when marks are also given" (19), which is what I found in my own experiences. Furthermore, according to Tomlinson and Moon (2013),

> First, a [grade] misrepresents the learning process to students leading them to conclude that making errors is cause for punishment rather than an opportunity to improve. Second, it focuses students more on getting good grades than on learning. Third, it makes the classroom environment seem unsafe for many students.
>
> (62)

In addition, Alfie Kohn suggests grades are invalid and unreliable in evaluating student learning, while Daniel Pink in *Drive: The Surprising Truth About What Motivates Us* says, "Good grades are a reward for compliance but don't have much to do with learning. Meanwhile, students whose grades don't measure up often see themselves as failures and give up trying to learn" (176).

I am sure you've met a student who has given up on trying because she's fallen behind due to absences or a student who has fallen behind even when she's shown up every day because she struggles or is uninspired. I kind of appreciate the student who resists. She knows the compliance game, and she is not playing it. We have to give these students a reason to show up, a reason to try or to inquire beyond "because this is school" or "because you'll fail" or "because I'll send you to the office."

As a punishment or as a reward, the grade is extrinsic to learning. Don't we want students to feel compelled, to be intrigued, to dare to imagine, to create? I am depending on these kids, our students, to fix the problems our generation has caused. I am counting on them to care about our world more than we did or at least better than we did.

It's All Formative: Ongoing Assessment

We have heard of formative assessment, and we know the importance of exit slips, anecdotal evidence, and checking notebooks to assess learning while students are practicing and exploring a new skill or concept. We do these assessments so that we can adjust instruction in order to improve learning (i.e., slow down, find another method, extend time). You may or may not assign grades to those formative assessments, but at the end of a unit or after teaching a set of skills or concepts, you perhaps give a test or assign a project. At that point, you likely assign a score or grade to a product or artifact. Why? Because grades are due? But has the learning stopped? And if a student does not complete the test or project, then what? And if the student fails the test, then what? And if the student is absent and does not come in during lunch to make up the work, then what?

When it comes to assessment, Alfie Kohn says,

> It matters whether the objective is to 1) rank kids against one another, 2) provide an extrinsic inducement for them to try harder, or 3) offer feedback that will help them become more adept at, and excited about, what they're doing.
>
> (15)

I want the shift in assessment to be toward feedback, which I will discuss in what follows. Simply put, "good" teaching is all about feedback. Ethical teaching is all about feedback through conversation. Keep the red pens in your desk, and stop taking home stacks of papers to "grade."

Narrative Feedback: Relating and Teaching Through Conversation

I have always tried to provide written narrative feedback—notes in the margin or at the end of a paper praising skills or suggesting revisions. It made sense with papers and portfolios to respond with notes to students about what I was noticing in their work. Ultimately, however, I assigned a grade, usually with some rubric and points, which always felt a little wrong—to quantify something that was/is beyond measurement, more than a number. Rubrics seemed like a rather just (and efficient) way of communicating expectations to students and their parents; however, I noticed rubrics becoming more of a way to justify the grades rather than making sense of how the skills supported the concepts and created new ideas. Essentially, rubrics work to standardize assignments and make students dependent on the rubric to do an assignment. Where is the innovation?

Maja Wilson in *Rethinking Rubrics in Writing Assessment* suggests teachers look at the product itself "to suggest its own evaluative criteria" (42). If by "product," Wilson means everything a student says and does, then, yes, teachers must engage with students while they are grappling, creating, thinking, and producing in order to provide feedback to stretch their learning. Any feedback—words, a score, a grade, a checklist—is rather useless once a product is complete (i.e., if there will be no opportunity to revise, reflect upon, extend the use of that product). To be clear, I am not suggesting that students do not do some culminating project like the multigenre research paper in the *Tree Girl* chapter or the memoir as they did in the witnessing chapter.

I am just saying that students' learning *is* in the process of making those artifacts, so that is when and where the feedback (or teaching) should happen. There is no need to put a number or letter on products because while there is evidence of the standards contained in those products, the products are merely a representation of a very complex process of learning, a process that you, the teacher, witnessed.

To sit alongside a student as she is reading and say, "Tell me about what you are reading. What do you think about that?" is quite different from standing in front of the class and saying, "Write your name on this worksheet; answer these questions; turn it in. It is worth 10 points." In the first, the teacher and students have a live encounter in which we don't know what the other might say. We will have to respond to each other and have a conversation about literature. The identity of "the teacher"—one who knows, who assigns, who grades—is superfluous in that conversation. In the learning conversation, the teacher is careful not to coerce the student to say or do what the teacher wants but is open to any response. In the second, we are asking for just the facts or a right answer. When a student completes the worksheet, but she has clearly missed a key component or can't quite do the skill, what do we do (if we are using traditional grades)? Subtract points, put a slash over the error, write a phrase like "awkward" or "do over." That is easier. That is controlled. That is standardizing because it minimizes diversity and marginalizes the students' individuality, humanity. This doesn't seem kind, helpful, or ethical, does it? A live encounter invites transformation—not standardization—of both teacher and student because the outcome is unknown and thus open to becoming.

If you have never talked to a student face to face about what she was learning, you might be wondering how to begin. Let's start with one assignment that I ask students to do typically once a week:

> Write a blog (or letter) about what you are reading. Start with a short summary so that we (your classmates and I) have some idea about what is going on in your book, and then talk about what you are noticing (a central question the book is exploring, an image that comes up again and again, a character's discoveries, how a theme has developed, the author's use of a supporting character, how the book is treating the subject—cliché or fresh). Include text evidence to support any claims you make using MLA citation. Finally, please include what you think about all this. I am interested in hearing why what you are noticing matters to you, to your understanding of the book, to your understanding of life.

Here is an example of a student's blog:

> I am currently reading *The Absolutely True Diary of a Part-Time Indian*. This book is about Arnold a boy with many different ability differences trying to get through high school outside of his Spokane reservation.

> Arnold joined the Reardon basketball team, but because of this he wanted to beat Rowdy (a rez "friend") in one of the games, stating "I want to beat Rowdy, I want to embarrass him" (182). This week I want to talk about is how Arnold changing schools affected the plot. For example, in one part it said, "The others at my rez call me an apple, red on the outside white on the Inside." (132). This shows that the others at home felt betrayed when they saw Arnold move schools, so they started to bully him more. The change affected Rowdy and Arnold friendship by hurting it; an example of this would be is when Rowdy hears the information he starts to cry but he hides it and then punches Arnold, giving him a black eye. After that Arnold repeatedly tries asking Rowdy for advice and tries to heal their friendship. This affects the plot by changing how Arnold thinks of Rowdy and how everyone treats him, but in Reardon people call him brave because of his choice. His family is not affected however.
>
> My question to you is how would you deal with everyone judging your decisions even if it's a good decision?

Now how would you respond to this student? In a learning conversation, you might explain what was done and give the student a chance to improve if the student did not demonstrate understanding of a standard or concept. Barnes suggests teachers assess student learning with a formula: SE2R: summarize, explain, redirect, and resubmit. I don't like the word *formula* in part because the letters remind me of grades, but it is easy to remember and apply in both written and verbal communication with students. Here is the SE2R in process:

- **Summarize:** Provide a one- or two-sentence summary of what students have accomplished on an activity or project. "You wrote a blog post about how Arnold's choice to change schools impacted the plot."
- **Explain:** Share detailed observations of what skills or concepts have been mastered based on the specific activity guidelines. "You clearly showed how characters responded to Arnold's decision. You identified passages where people at the rez responded with harsh words and actions and how some people at the new school treat him with respect. You also use MLA citation to include text evidence."
- **Redirect:** Indicate for students the lessons, presentations, or models that need to be reviewed in order to achieve understanding of concepts or skills. "I wonder about your last sentence, saying his family was not affected. I thought that Arnold's decision did seem to impact his sister's choice to also leave the rez, and I think Arnold's decision to go off the rez for school impacted his family. What do you think? Can you find those passages?"
- **Resubmit:** Encourage students to rework activities after revisiting prior learning, and resubmit them for further feedback. "After thinking about the impact Arnold's decision had on his family and rereading a few passages, revise or add on to your blog."

Any teacher who uses a writing workshop approach recognizes components of this formula. When you conference with a student, you summarize what you heard, explain a strategy, suggest revisions, and then check in to see the next draft. And if you have tried a reading workshop, then you do this, too—especially if students are blogging or keeping a reading journal. You are teaching through conversation. You are treating your students as human beings capable of talking about their learning as something that is ongoing rather than "finished" at some arbitrary point. And when we assign a grade, we essentially end the conversation.

Early on, when I started this conversation approach to assessment, students would ask me, "What is my grade?" I replied, "This conversation takes the place of the grade; instead of a letter or a number, it is in the form of a few sentences and invites you to deepen and stretch what you are learning and discovering." They usually responded with a quizzical look. For me, the "resubmit" part does not always happen because our conversations are applied to the next reading event or blog. I ask students to either write me a note at the bottom of their blog post or just to tell me in our next conference what they are doing differently or how they are building on our conversations about a standard (e.g., text evidence, theme development) or a concept (e.g., how authors represent atrocities in narratives).

To be clear, standards do guide my instruction. However, the curriculum of my course, any English course, goes far beyond any list of standards. What I am emphasizing here is that our aim should not be any sort of standardization of process or product. For now, I create assignments that start and continue learning conversations like blogs, discussion groups, speeches, films, and research projects, but I am working toward making the classroom a space where students will begin to propose what they will read, research, write, do, or create and where I will be but one resource in their realization of that process. I am only beginning to imagine the possibilities of an education that would move students to take such initiative.

For now, my feedback is the best resource I have. I use written narrative feedback occasionally, but for the most part, my feedback happens face to face, human to human. For example, for an assignment like the quoted blog post, sometimes I do write feedback, but I prefer to offer similar feedback verbally during reading workshop time. When I followed up with this student about his reading of Alexie's work, I found that he indeed noticed the impact of Arnold's decision (to leave the rez) on his family, but what is even better is that we reread that section together and had a short but deep conversation about the passage. Conversation is not only evidence of students' reading but evidence of how a student is engaging with the ideas of the book and how that student can communicate interpretations with another human being: me (or other readers). I have read Alexie's novel many times, and I bring to it my life and the lives of students with whom I have read the novel, but in that moment, I have never read the book with that student at that time, and we are both transformed in that encounter.

There Is Enough Time

I teach six classes of 25 to 30 students: 180. Now there is a number. Not all feedback (or better yet assessment) has to be written. I keep a clipboard for me and the teachers with whom I co-teach to mark when we've conferred with students about certain standards or concepts. I don't make it around to talk to every student every day, but in the course of a week, I come close, and for the students I don't encounter in person, I write on their blogs, send an email, comment in their Google Drive project, or chat with them through our Remind account. The blogs work as a portfolio of student work, quarterly reflections, recordings of book groups, letters to parents about learning, and my written feedback. I do not take home papers to "grade" anymore. My work happens in the classroom. Sure, I comment on blogs and emails outside of class, but that is nothing compared to the hours I would spend alone "grading," writing comments of little use to the students.

Report Cards Are a Necessary Conversation (for Now)

I still have to contend with quarterly report cards even though my principal is supporting this pilot year. The school district requires a letter grade at the end of the term. This is problematic because a quarter or term grade averages learning experiences. The letter does not tell the story of weeks of learning conversations with teachers and peers. Barnes suggests the final grade ought to be decided based on a "detailed assessment by both teacher and student of all that was or was not accomplished during a grading period" (5). My principal has agreed to conferencing final grades, but his concern was how to communicate this process to parents who, like students, see the teacher as the authority.

Before the grade conference, I ask students to look through their projects, writing, notes, blogs, and any written feedback I've offered and then compose a "summary of learning" that we use for our end-of-term grade conference. What did you do this term? What did you learn? How do you know? (Although it is too lengthy to include here, you can see an example of a "summary of learning" on my blog, Ethical ELA, at http://www.ethicalela.com/.) When it comes to conferring for a final grade, I explain as best I can that the letter does not define the student, that one letter cannot tell the story of learning. We start with these descriptors and negotiate a grade from there:

- I can show evidence of the concepts we've studied this term (e.g., what makes a classic, how are ability differences represented, cliché endings, the problem of historical fiction).
- I can explain how I am using standards in the service of those concepts (e.g., text evidence, theme development, coming to group prepared, working with diverse partners, using technology to collaborate).

- I have accepted/considered feedback and revised my artifacts to stretch and extend my thinking (e.g., blogs, discussions, book selections, reading practice, films, essays).
- I can give evidence that I am not just complying with assignments but that I go beyond assignment descriptors and even propose experiences to help me process and show my learning.
- I can articulate how our reading experiences are impacting thinking about reading, literature, classmates, and the world.

In our grade conferences, we talk through these descriptors, which are not comprehensive but do get close to valuing a learning as a process with a balance of content, standards, experiences, autonomy, and reflection. For the most part, students know where they are with regard to a grade. They know if they are missing evidence or not going beyond, they are likely not in the A–B range. I try to be available and open to hearing what I can do better to engage them in their learning or if we need help from parents or even social workers to problem solve. Only a few students will "fail" when learning conversations are at the heart of your teaching because the conversations are evidence of learning.

The conferences are working well for me now. To get started, I have found it helpful to show students a sample video of a grade conference and have them practice with each other so that our teacher–student conferences are meaningful and efficient. If you have a class of twenty-five or thirty, you will need to set aside a week for this, which means if you have a nine-week quarter, you will spend the entire last week conferencing, so that week is a good time for a student-led project. For parents, I send home or email students' written "summary of learning" to supplement their grade report.

I want my students to take ownership of their learning, but I still hear students ask: *What is my grade?* I usually just ask them to tell me what they think and then follow up with my own question: *How do you know?* When it comes to conversations among teachers and administrators, we still talk about GPAs, but we are also talking about students who are genuinely struggling to engage with school and get involved with their learning.

Learning conversations and grade conferences are two ways I am trying to minimize standardization in my classroom. I realize that public schools are not the boarding schools of the past, but accountability and fear of failure to meet can create conditions that make teachers and students give up their "songs and stories and language and dancing"—the very diversity our world needs (Alexie 35).

Conclusion

In May of 2015, Governor Jay Inslee signed into Washington State's law a mandate that will teach a tribal sovereignty curriculum. In a study of nearly two thousand K–12 standards, researchers found, "Ninety percent of the texts taught were written by non-Natives" and "87 percent of all the curriculum had erased or forgotten indigenous people after the year 1900" (Brownstone). Before the mandate, students did not learn about boarding schools and attempts to erase Native cultures, religions, and languages from the United States. This mandate attempts to correct such omissions. Indeed, as we have seen with the genocide education mandates, states can require teachers to teach and students to then know about something, but I have been suggesting that our work goes beyond knowledge accumulation. To know about is one thing, but to confront, to intervene, to act is something quite different. We have to get closer to an education that moves students to ask: What do I do with this knowing? If we give them a test and mark it with a letter or number, we may be answering this question for our students.

Rethinking assessment means rethinking this idea of accountability. For what are we accounting in our classrooms? When it comes to learning, a number or letter might be a form of counting learning or accounting for effort, compliance, or meeting a standard, but such marks tend to end conversations about learning. Rethinking assessment is about positioning the student as the authority on their learning experience. Minimizing scoring and grades makes space for the student to ask new questions. Instead of asking "What is my grade?" you will hear students ask, "What can I do now?" And you may even hear, instead of a question, "Here is what I want to learn [or do or create]."

Works Cited

Alexie, Sherman. *The Absolutely True Diary of a Part-Time Indian*. New York: Little, Brown, and Co., 2007. Print.

Barnes, Mark. *Assessment 3.0: Throw Out Your Grade Book and Inspire Learning*. Thousand Oaks, CA: Corwin, 2015. Print.

Brownstone, Sydney. "Teaching Tribal History is Finally Required in Washington Public Schools." *The Stranger*. 24 June 1015. Web.

"Dreams and Schemes." *Into the West*. Steven Spielberg, Director. TNT. 10 June 2005. Television.

Kohn, Alfie. "The Trouble with Rubrics." *English Journal*. 95.4 (March 2006): 12–15. Web.

Pink, Daniel H. *Drive: The Surprising Truth About What Motivates Us*. New York: Riverhead Books, 2009. Print.

Sackstein, Starr. *Hacking Assessment: 10 Ways to Go Gradeless in a Traditional Grades School*. Cleveland, OH: Times 10 Publications, 2015. Print.

Tomlinson, Carol A., and Tonya R. Moon. *Assessment and Student Success in a Differentiated Classroom*. Alexandria, VA: ASCD, 2013. Web.

Wilson, Maja. *Rethinking Rubrics in Writing Assessment*. Portsmouth, NH: Heinemann, 2006. Print.

Literature for Your Classroom Library, Native Peoples of North America

Debbie Reese established American Indians in Children's Literature (AICL) in 2006 to provide critical perspectives and analysis of Indigenous peoples in children's and young adult books and school curriculum. She is tribally enrolled at Nambe Pueblo in northern New Mexico. She holds a doctorate in education and a master's in library science and taught elementary school in public schools and in two schools for American Indians: Riverside Indian School in Anadarko, Oklahoma, and Santa Fe Indian School in New Mexico. Here she offers book recommendations for your classroom:

> An honest examination of the history of the United States would include many examples in which European and U.S. leaders committed acts of genocide against Native peoples. While some history textbooks gesture towards those acts, they are generally omitted. Teachers who want to bring them to students can turn to books by Native writers. Here's three examples:
>
>> Tim Tingle's *How I Became a Ghost* is about the removal of the Choctaw Nation from its homelands in 1830. Commonly referenced today as the Trail of Tears, the brutality with which Native peoples were rounded up and held in pens as they waited to be marched during harsh conditions to Indian Territory, and the deaths of people during that march, are an example of "causing serious bodily or mental harm to members of the group." The main character in Tingle's book is a ten-year-old boy named Isaac who will die during the march, but remain in the story as a ghost.
>>
>> "Imposing measures intended to prevent births within the group" is the subject of Joseph Bruchac's *Hidden Roots.* In it, 11-year-old Harold learns he is Abenaki, but that his family has kept their Native identity secret to protect themselves. Set in the 1960s, Bruchac's book is about the sterilization of Native people through state sanctioned research projects known by names such as Building Better Vermonters.
>>
>> In Shirley Stirling's *My Name Is Seepeetza*, readers learn about "forcibly transferring children of the group to another group" by way of federal boarding schools in the United States and Canada whose goal was to "kill the Indian and save the man." Set in the 1950s in British Columbia, Stirling's autobiographical novel about being in the school is presented from the point of view of a sixth grade girl.

Brownstone, Sydney. "Teaching Tribal History Is Finally Required in Washington Public Schools." *The Stranger.* 24 Jun 2015. Web.

Bruchac, Joseph. *Hidden Roots*. New York: Scholastic, 2004. Print.

Edwardson, Debby D., Alex Ferrari, and Melanie Kroupa. *My Name Is Not Easy*. New York: Marshall Cavendish, 2011. Print.

Gansworth, Eric L. *If I Ever Get Out of Here: A Novel with Paintings*. New York: Arthur A. Levine Books, 2013. Print.

Leatherdale, Mary B., and Lisa Charleyboy. *Urban Tribes: Native Americans in the City*. Toronto, Ontario: Annick Press, 2015. Print.

Marshall, Joseph, and Jim Yellowhawk. *In the Footsteps of Crazy Horse*. New York: Amulet Books, 2015. Print.
Smith, Cynthia L. *Rain Is Not My Indian Name*. New York: HarperCollins, 2001. Print.
Sterling, Shirley. *My Name Is Seepeetza*. Vancouver: Douglas & McIntyre, 1992. Print.
Tingle, Tim. *House of Purple Cedar*. El Paso, TX: Puntos Press, 2014. Print.
Tingle, Tim. *How I Became a Ghost: A Choctaw Trail of Tears Story*. Oklahoma City, OK: The RoadRunner Press, 2013. Print.
Tingle, Tim. *No Name*. Summertown, TN: 7th Generation, 2014. Print.

A Teacher's Testimony

Amy Estanislao is a high school English teacher in Chicago Public Schools. Here Amy considers how best to balance ethical assessment practices with high-stakes testing:

> After reading about genocide with my students for the last two years, I have realized the importance of focusing our learning on expanding our worldview. It can be so easy to get caught up in reading texts in which the students can so closely identify with the characters or the classic texts form the cannon. However, it is also important to expose students to the unfamiliar world around them. I believe that it is important for the students to be informed members of the world community in order to be able to take part in the daily conversations that happen around them.
>
> In order to accomplish this quite lofty goal, I realized that reading, engaging in activities, and taking a test was not an authentic or accurate way to assess student learning. Instead, I try to spend our time engaging in conversations and encouraging students to demonstrate their learning through more authentic assessments such as multigenre inquiry projects. Instead of ending our units with final tests, we engage in activities in which the students try to further their understanding of the topics we explore. When we study how stereotypes impact our society and everyday life, the students examine the implicit and explicit messages that are constantly acting upon them through multiple modes of media. The students then take it a step further by proposing ways in which to fight those stereotypical messages.
>
> Although I try my best to incorporate these more authentic modes of assessment into my curriculum, it is still difficult to balance preparing students to take standardized tests. It is hard to ignore the impending spring testing season. My students are going to be expected to

log onto a computer and navigate an overwhelming and confusing test structure. Although I have confidence that through the variety of alternative assessments we have engaged in we've prepared the students to answer the questions on the test, the navigating of the test alone is an obstacle. Therefore, I do utilize an online reading program that has a similar setup. I do not use this in isolation, but more as a supplement to my curriculum. I believe that this balance has been the most ethical way of assessing and teaching my students.

It is my hope that these ways of engaging with texts will encourage students to be more active in their learning. I want my students to constantly question and think of the ways they can broaden their understanding of the world. By being active participants in their learning, they are hopefully learning how to be able to initiate change.

13 Conclusion

The Education of a Teacher Continues

> Reading the world always precedes reading the word, and reading the word implies continually reading the world . . . [W]e can go further and say that reading the word is not preceded by merely reading the world, but by a certain form of *writing* it or *rewriting* it, that is, of transforming it by means of conscious, practical work.
>
> —Paulo Freire, *Literacy: Reading the Word and the World*

I became an English teacher because I believe literature has the potential to enrich the lives of human beings, to build a capacity of sympathy for others, to invite inquiry into dimensions of society that we may overlook in our day-to-day lives, and ultimately to move us to be more ethical members of society. I asked at the beginning of this book: How might students be educated to confront inhumanity instead of collaborating with it through action or inaction? In writing this book, I have sought to answer that question for the English classroom by considering what *ought* to happen in the English classroom, and in doing so, I have reconnected with what brought me to teaching English: students and their stories.

I have explored ethical reading and teaching in English classrooms of middle and secondary schools, and I have shared a few of my own experiences of reading genocide literature to show its incompatibility with standards and accountability, but this has all been about the students.

In pursuing rhetoric, witnessing, and social action in my own practice, the rhetoric of progress in education—that new standards and new testing will close the achievement gap and make students college and career ready—and threats of accountability continue to coax me into data analysis and interrupt my curriculum with hours of testing. I am tempted by the teaching guides administrators put in my mailbox that promise Common Core State Standards alignment. However, such challenges have proven to be opportunities to illuminate in the classroom the darker side of progress and the way institutions and policies perpetuate certain values, marginalize certain experiences, and ultimately attempt to constrain innovation. In other words, as Paulo Freire suggests, teachers and students can "rewrite" the world, can transform it "by means of conscious, practical work." And every day, in room H103, this is what I *try* to do as a middle school teacher in my six classes and with my 180 students.

I propose in this book an approach to reading that sees the process of meaning making in the spaces where the story of a text's creation interacts with the story of the reader and her community of readers. I have emphasized that meaning making is a dynamic process that resists measurement. Readers practice becoming conscious of the multitude of actions that shape or attempt to color our understanding of the world and our place in it. The "becoming" is not a finite state of being, but it can be practiced; it can be nurtured with guidance; and it is observable in the classroom; it is just not quantifiable.

Teachers have an ethical responsibility to teach reading in such a way that students can saturate their consciousness in opportunities to learn their epistemological and ethical responsibility to the text and, in the case of testimonial literature, the witness. I have argued that teaching genocide literature, in particular, illuminates some ethical issues with reading practices that suggest there is a "right" reading or that a "good" reader is someone who earns a certain score on high-stakes tests. Did Elie Wiesel write *Night* as a tool for teaching symbolism? No. He wrote it to justify his own survival and to initiate as many encounters as possible with his readers, those who bear witness to his testimony.

I discussed genocide literature to emphasize the importance of ethical reading and teaching because texts that represent genocide ask us, as human beings who share this world, to face *the* gorgons (Levi; Clendinnen). The word "gorgon" derives from the Greek *gorgós*, meaning dreadful. In Greek literature, Gorgons were female dragon-like creatures with wings whose hair was made of living, venomous snakes. In modern times, fantasy books depict Gorgons as "evil monsters whose biggest weapon is their appearance of normalcy and beauty"; Medusa, the queen of the Gorgons, could "turn people to stone with a stare" (Sjoberg and Gentry 38). To face the Gorgon of genocide means to look at it, to attempt some understanding of the conditions that perpetuate it, and to ultimately cut off the oppression and injustice that numb society to the distant suffering of others. Genocide literature asks us to face genocide: to name it, to witness it, to acknowledge our capacity for such hatred. I am also asking us to face the systems, traditions, and practices that marginalize students' voices and experiences and stifle students' capacity to read beyond the classroom.

As teachers of the word and the world, we are teaching our students to confront the many gorgons they will face in their lives, and we want them to do so with consciousness, with a strong sense of ethics, and with courage. Any teacher who has read Mikaelsen's *Tree Girl*, Ung's *First They Killed My Father*, Combres's *Broken Memory*, or Alexie's *The Absolutely True Diary of a Part-Time Indian* alongside her students knows that students, even as young as middle school, are not only curious about the violence in the world but have a deep desire to understand how crimes against humanity are possible in our modern world. Students have very strong ideas for how society *ought* to be. Our students want to face the gorgons of our world, but they need our support in resisting the urge to turn away or, perhaps worse, to stave off apathy.

As teachers, this means that we have to lead the way first by facing the gorgons of twenty-first-century education. We have to take a look at the rhetoric of public education and ask questions about the way these new standards and high-stakes tests are infiltrating our curriculum and pedagogy. Our classrooms must be places to uncover what is and imagine what can be. And for these reason, I regard this book as an important academic accomplishment. This book has been my way of facing the gorgons that threaten public education and English curriculum and pedagogy, but ultimately it is about my becoming a better teacher and human being.

As I discussed throughout this book, education is much more than "college and career ready." We and our students are agents of memory who will take the memories of our lives and the memories we create alongside one another in our classrooms out into the world. If students consider the purpose of education to be preparing them for college and careers without some framework of consciousness, they may go out into the world and perpetuate the structures that foster oppression and violence in the world. English teachers have an important role in guiding young readers by teaching an awareness of rhetoricality, cultivating a way of being with others that sees listening as witnessing, and encouraging an imagination for how things *ought* to be.

For more than a decade, I have witnessed teachers doing *good* work often closing their doors on the latest school initiative for the sake of their students. And I have worked with principals who have innovative ways for working within otherwise restrictive mandates for the sake of their teachers and students. I have been fortunate in recent years to work with principals who have encouraged me to develop my practice because, despite reform efforts, we haven't seen the achievement gap close and because what Lincoln's community needs cannot be measured in data or found in some new, aligned textbook. They've supported my efforts to get more books about global issues, to teach about human rights, and to read without bubbles to shade or blanks to fill. For me, it has been a privilege to sit alongside Lincoln's students as they feel, ponder, deliberate, question, and even judge the art and ethics of genocide literature specifically, but literature more broadly.

Unfortunately, I know that my experiences are not necessarily shared by other teachers at Lincoln and perhaps in other schools. Some English teachers at Lincoln do not think that teaching about genocide is their job, and while they complied with the district's decision for the English and history departments to share the responsibility of meeting the Illinois Genocide Education Mandate (to different extents) in 2005, the new Common Core State Standards (CCSS) have teachers looking for curriculum to cut in order to meet the demands of the new standards and state test.

As recent as the spring of 2013 (eight years after the Illinois Genocide Education Mandate), I was copied on an email sent to the principal from a teacher who essentially said that because of the new CCSS, they would no longer have time to teach a genocide unit *and* cover all the new state standards. After a decade of shifting to a more globally conscious curriculum and developing a library of genocide literature, the CCSS nearly undid it all. While the principal did not accept this email as the final word on the issue, two issues became apparent: first, it seemed that anxiety over the CCSS and teacher accountability measures may have led some English teachers to interpret (misinterpret) the standards *as* curriculum, and second, the debate over which discipline should have the burden (or privilege) of meeting the state mandate, which began in 2005, was never fully resolved.

To respond to the first, the CCSS do not indicate what students should read at which grade level but rather outline learning objectives; for example, according to Common Core State Standards' website, two seventh-grade standards in reading literature include the following: "cite several pieces of textual evidence to support analysis of what the text says explicitly as well as inferences drawn from the text" (7.1) and "compare and contrast a fictional portrayal of a time, place, or character and a historical account of the same period as a means of understanding how authors of fiction use or alter history" (7.9). Reading any number of novels about genocide would support these standards while also meeting the genocide mandate, at minimum. However, the rhetoric of CCSS is such that some teachers are interpreting them as curriculum.

In an article on perspectives of CCSS, Jory Brass argues, "the CCSS normalize certain curricular aims (global economic competition, college and career readiness), encourage certain kinds of educational experiences (text-dependent questions, behavioral objectives, high-stakes testing), and name standards as ordering principles to legitimate, discipline, and control classroom practice" (Savage, O'Connor, and Brass 23–24). The teaching guides distributed widely by school districts alongside new teacher evaluation procedures have moved teachers to drastically change curriculum and methods without understanding the implications of the standards or validity of the new tests, which may take up to 11 hours to complete (Gewertz). In just its first year, the CCSS are disciplining practices of curriculum and pedagogy (Brass). However, in my view, English teachers concerned about the new standards, high-stakes testing, and teacher evaluations can read testimonial literature, genocide novels, photographs, and films with students and still address the learning objectives stated in the CCSS. The CCSS calls for complex texts and primary source documents that promote "rigorous conversations" and for assessments with "text-dependent questions." English teachers can do all this without the new CCSS–aligned guides and textbooks. In other words, rather ironically, I want English teachers to read and even apply the CCSS, but we have to do so in ways that make space for students' aesthetic responses, for conversations that elicit multiple, valid interpretations, for inquiry into the rhetoricality of these texts (including CCSS), for opportunities to bear witness, and for imagining what *ought* to be. And we have to consider ways we frame or structure our class time in addition to our assessment and grading practices, which are all bound up in oppressive systems of measurement.

To respond to the second, it seems to me that the English teachers in my school, and perhaps elsewhere, still—after nearly twenty-five years since the Holocaust education mandate and a decade since the genocide education mandate—consider genocide education as a strictly historical project, not a literacy or literary project. The chapters on witnessing illustrate the value of reading testimonial literature with English students, and the chapters on fiction offer an argument for reading genocide novels with English students, but ideally, English teachers and history teachers would collaborate as a way of investigating the nature of historical knowledge and the function of historical writing. I hope that my work thus far has demonstrated how my own study has been enriched by many reading experiences not only among literary and historical texts but within and across conversations with teachers, students, and witnesses. In my view, uncovering and preventing genocidal processes is not an endeavor for English or history; it is or should be an education endeavor. We are teaching students first and foremost.

While elevating the academic concern of reading theories and genocide literature with good intention, I maintain a critical perspective to detect the issues and ruptures in this particular approach. As I have been discussing the ethics of teaching and learning in a progress, systems-oriented, measurement-focused society, and as I have put forth a way of reading genocide literature to encourage all readers to be conscious of the transactions that shape and transform our world, some may see this theory as a sort of pedagogical mandate. I want to note that I have not suggested we abandon altogether an inquiry into the methods and systems that have constrained reading practices and thus learning, nor have I suggested we replace the new reading standards. Instead, I have been suggesting that the English classroom read in such a way as to illuminate all agents, transactions, and contexts and to be conscious of how all texts teach us to see others, the world, and our place in it.

While I have argued for rhetoric, witnessing, and social action when reading genocide literature, I imagine some readers will see this book as limited to reading genocide literature and, perhaps, disregard it when reading other genres. However, I hope my readers will see the potential of this approach in reading more broadly, including nontextual mediums such as images and films.

In concluding at this point, I realize that this project has been primarily theoretical and that some issues of practical application remain unresolved. For example, I realize that some teachers are looking for a lesson plan or a step-by-step approach to how to teach "rhetoricality" or "witnessing." I hesitate to offer such guides because I see ethical reading as a philosophy of teaching and want to resist constraining how other teachers may interpret my ideas into their own practice. That said, the few stories from my practice that I have included in this book offer readers some insight into how I am working toward more ethical methods in this time of standards and accountability. Perhaps my stories may serve as inspiration for other English teachers who are reimagining what the English classroom can do and be for our students.

This ending note is in essence not a conclusion. Instead, it is rather an ongoing statement proclaiming that as a teacher, I am always becoming. By completing this work, I am looking forward to seeing more scholars and teachers participate in the development of ethical reading practices. After more than a decade of teaching, I have come to realize that while students enjoy and benefit from reading literature that might mirror their lives to some degree, I think they also want literature that asks them to engage with distant others. I think students want to understand how texts and images move them, to practice their epistemological and ethical responsibilities, and to imagine what their world, our world, *ought* to be. As Maxine Greene reminds me and my fellow teachers, "We must have in mind a quest for a better state of things for those we teach and for the world we all teach. It is simply not enough to reproduce the way things are" (1).

Works Cited

Clendinnen, Inga. *Reading the Holocaust.* Cambridge, UK: Cambridge University Press, 1999. Print.

English Language Arts Standards. Common Core State Standards Initiative. 27 Oct. 2012. Web.

Freire, Paulo, and Donald P. Macedo. *Literacy: Reading the Word and the World.* South Hadley, MA: Bergin & Garvey, 1987. Print.

Gewertz, Catherine. "Common-Core Assessment Group Revises Testing Time." *Education Week.org.* 25 Sept. 2014. Web.

Greene, Maxine. *Releasing the Imagination: Essays on Education, the Arts, and Social Change.* San Francisco: Jossey-Bass, 1995. Print.

Levi, Primo. *If This Is a Man and the Truce.* London: Little, Brown Book Group, 1991. Print.

Savage, Glenn C., Kate O'Connor, and Jory Brass. "Perspectives: Common Core State Standards, Implications for Curriculum, Equality, and Policy." *Journal of Curriculum and Pedagogy.* 11.1. (2014). 18–49. Print.

Sjoberg, Laura, and Caron E. Gentry. *Mothers, Monsters, Whores: Women's Violence in Global Politics.* New York: Zed Books, 2007. Print.

Index

Page numbers in *italics* refer to figures.

For Product Safety Concerns and Information please contact our EU representative GPSR@taylorandfrancis.com
Taylor & Francis Verlag GmbH, Kaufingerstraße 24, 80331 München, Germany

www.ingramcontent.com/pod-product-compliance
Ingram Content Group UK Ltd.
Pitfield, Milton Keynes, MK11 3LW, UK
UKHW021300190926
475701UK00009B/89
* 9 7 8 1 1 3 8 3 1 5 3 7 2 *